Becoming a Practitioner in the Early Years

Becoming a Practitioner in the Early Years

Rose Envy
Rebecca Walters

Learning Matters
An imprint of SAGE Publications Ltd
1 Oliver's Yard
55 City Road
London EC1Y 1SP

SAGE Publications Inc.
2455 Teller Road
Thousand Oaks, California 91320

SAGE Publications India Pvt Ltd
B1/I 1 Mohan Cooperative Industrial Area
Mathura Road
New Delhi 110 044

SAGE Asia-Pacific Pte Ltd
3 Church Street
#10-04 Samsung Hub
Singapore 049483

Editor: Amy Thornton
Development editor: Geoff Barker
Production controller: Chris Marke
Project management: Deer Park Productions,
Tavistock, Devon
Marketing manager: Catherine Slinn
Cover design: Wendy Scott
Typeset by: PDQ Typesetting Ltd
Printed and bound by MPG Printgroup, UK

MIX
Paper from
responsible sources
FSC® C018575

Library of Congress Control Number:
2013932597

British Library Cataloguing in Publication data

A catalogue record for this book is available
from the British Library.

ISBN 978 1 44626 793 6 (hbk) and
978 1 44626 794 3 (pbk)

Contents

The authors

Rose Envy is Senior Lecturer in Education at Teesside University. She is programme leader for the BA (Hons) Children and Early Childhood degree and acts as Examination and Assessment Officer for the Education Department within the School of Social Sciences and Law. Rose spent the early part of her career in nursing, later moving to a career in early years education. Rose has worked for local authorities at a strategic level, developing the early years workforce. She has also worked in partnership with universities in the region to develop new qualifications for the children's workforce at both undergraduate and postgraduate level. Her specialist area is leadership and management, with interests in childhood poverty and the effect this has upon families both in terms of improving outcomes for children and families and inter-family relationships.

Rebecca Walters has a background in early years teaching within schools – Foundation and Key Stages 1 and 2. She graduated from Bishop Grosseteste University College Lincoln with a BA (Hons) Primary Education degree which incorporated a Qualified Teacher Status. While teaching she completed an MA Education. It was an action research degree which means it was research oriented towards enhancing direct practice. After 13 years within primary schools, Rebecca's passion for learning brought her to Teesside University. Rebecca is currently a senior lecturer in Education at Teesside University. She also teaches on the MA in Education, Childhood and Youth, and delivers the Early Years Professional Status. She is also the Year 2 tutor for the BA (Hons) Early Childhood Studies.

Martin Harmer has worked in combined children's centres and family centres in London and Bradford before training as a social worker and working for the NSPCC investigating concerns about children, assessing abuse situations and providing therapeutic work with children and families. He is currently a Senior Lecturer at Teesside University on the early years/education team. His academic interests are in early intervention, child protection and safeguarding, and family support.

Acknowledgements

Every effort has been made to trace the copyright holders and to obtain their permission for the use of copyright material. The publisher and author will gladly receive any information enabling them to rectify any error or omission in subsequent editions.

Introduction

The intention of this book is to provide you with an overview of the different aspects of early years practice and provide an opportunity for you to reflect upon the knowledge and skills you will need to acquire to become a successful early years practitioner. Whatever career aspirations you may have, we hope that this book will be the starting block from which you can build your knowledge and understanding of the various aspects of early years practice. We wish you well in your studies and hope that you achieve your goal.

Chapter summaries

Chapter 1: Developing the children's workforce

This chapter will provide the rationale for the book and will discuss the policy developments which have led to the development of a dynamic and diverse children's workforce of which early years is an integral part. It will discuss issues around the need to develop a children's workforce which is equipped to meet the needs of children across a range of children's services. The chapter will encourage students to critically reflect upon the common core of skills and knowledge in relation to their practice.

Chapter 2: Collaborative working within early years

This chapter will provide a brief overview of the policy developments which have led to the development of integrated working practices. It will provide you with an opportunity to reflect upon the skills required to work within a multi-disciplinary team. It will identify examples of good practice and the challenges of multi-agency working. The chapter will encourage students to critically reflect upon their own skills and areas for development.

Chapter 3: Developing child-centred practices

This chapter will provide a brief overview of the history of early years education. It looks at the development of thinking around how children learn and what kind of environment encourages this learning. This is the starting point for thinking about education in early years, the role of play in learning and how practitioners can best support children in their learning.

Chapter 4: Pedagogy

This chapter will consider the term pedagogy in its broadest sense and consider how we understand it. This will provide you with the opportunity to consider your own pedagogy and the influences from your own educational background that have impacted on how you approach working with and supporting young children. To help explain this autobiographical accounts have been used examining how my own experiences of education have influenced my own developing pedagogy. You should consider key aspects from your background and use these to develop an understanding of the foundations of your own beliefs about your role in education.

Chapter 5: Enhancing pedagogical practice

This chapter will build on the previous chapter, probing in greater depth the specific elements that enhance practice with young children. In earlier chapters we considered how historical and political influences have shaped and moulded the curriculum within the early years sector into what it is today. The defining factor in the early years is the role of play in developing, supporting and enhancing learning. This chapter will consider how practitioners plan for and support play in the curriculum and some of the difficulties with this. It will also consider the role of the environment in supporting children's learning, considering this as a crucial element in developing an optimum learning space to enable children to learn through a mix of child-initiated play and adult-led play. The chapter will consider the nature of observations and assessments in planning and supporting children's learning. The role of parent partnerships will be explored, focusing on examples of good practice with an emphasis on parents as a child's first educator and the impact this has on enhancing the learning for young children.

Chapter 6: Becoming a reflective practitioner

This chapter will consider the terms 'reflection' and 'reflective practice'. It will provide you with the opportunity to consider how the processes of deep and thoughtful reflection can develop and support your practice through constructive critical examination of actions and outcomes. The chapter will encourage you to consider aspects of practice and use a range of different reflective models to progress through a reflective process, making links between the theory of reflection and the evaluation and improvement of practice in action.

Chapter 7: Creating inclusive environments

This chapter will explore the notion of inclusive practice, firstly by discussing the legislative framework which guides early years practice, and secondly by critically reflecting upon the inclusivity of early years practices. It will provide the student with an opportunity to reflect upon the skills required to provide an inclusive early years environment. The chapter will encourage students to critically reflect upon their own skills and areas for development.

Chapter 8: Ensuring safe practice

This chapter will provide a brief overview of recent policy directions relevant to safeguarding and child protection. It will provide an opportunity to reflect on the skills required to work effectively in this area with children, parents and carers, and other professionals. We will consider how good management practice can effectively support staff to maximise the safety and well-being of all children in the setting (universal safeguarding). We will briefly summarise the key procedures and actions which need to be taken where children are more vulnerable (targeted safeguarding), and explore the skills necessary to contribute effectively with other agencies, as part of wider assessment/investigation or work to support children and families following abuse (responsive safeguarding).

Chapter 9: The aspiring leader: taking your practice further

This chapter will explore early years leadership in the context of workforce reform. It will provide practitioners with an opportunity to reflect upon the skills required to become an effective leader in early years by making explicit the link between personal skills and the standards aligned to Early Years Practitioner Status. Students will be encouraged to explore the definition between leadership and management and reflect upon the skills required to become effective leaders and managers of early years settings. The chapter will also provide an opportunity for practitioners to identify areas for personal development.

1 Developing the children's workforce

Rose Envy

Reading through this chapter will help you to:

- reflect upon your own role in relation to the wider children's workforce;
- critically appraise the skills required to work with children across a range of children's services;
- apply your understanding of the skills required to work with children in relation to early years and identify those skills you need to develop further.

Introduction: the early years practitioner and the wider children's workforce

The intention of this book is to provide you with an overview of the different aspects of early years practice and provide an opportunity for you to reflect upon the knowledge and skills you will need to acquire to become a successful early years practitioner. This chapter will enable you to consider the role of the early years practitioner within the context of the wider children's workforce. Studying on an early childhood studies degree provides you with the skills and knowledge to be able to enter the children's workforce across a range of services.

ACTIVITY 1

Think of the term 'the children's workforce'. What do we mean by this? Is the term said in reference only to those who work with young children, or does it include all those who work indirectly with children and their families?

The children's workforce does not refer only to those practitioners who work in early years or teaching. All those who work with children, young people and their families are an integral part of the children's workforce. The DCSF (2008e, p3) states that:

> *Everyone who works with a child or young person or with their family has a role to play in supporting their development across all five Every Child Matters outcomes – whether they work in education, health, 14–19 learning, safety and crime prevention, out-of-school activities, child care, play, community involvement or economic wellbeing.*

To give you a better understanding of the range of roles within the children's workforce, Table 1.1 identifies many of the roles within each of the different services.

Table 1.1 The children's workforce

The children's workforce	Core workforce	Wider workforce
Early years	Managers, deputies, assistants and workers in: • playgroups • children's centres • day nurseries • nursery schools • nursery classes in primary schools • registered childminders and nannies	
Managers and leaders	Planners Housing and transport providers/ commissioners HR in organisations that provide services to children/young people	Strategic, senior and middle managers in all Children's Trust partner organisations All commissioners of services for children and/or young people
Education	Head teachers Teachers' school support staff Providers of extended schools activities Learning mentors Behaviour and educational support teams 14–19 providers Educational psychologists Educational welfare officers School meal staff	Staff and leaders of FE colleges Adult and community education providers
Health	Health visitors School nurses Community children's nurses Sick children's nurses Child psychologists Paediatricians Community paediatricians Children's allied health professionals Teenage pregnancy workers	GPs Primary and community health practitioners Clinical practitioners General medical and dental practitioners Hospitals Community health services Sexual health services Drugs and alcohol services Adult mental health services

The children's workforce	Core workforce	Wider workforce
Social, family and community support	Children and families social workers CAFCASS advisers Foster carers Private foster carers Outreach and family support workers Managers and staff in: • family centres • day centres • residential children's homes Portage workers Play workers	Parenting practitioners Adult social care workers Supporting People teams Drug and alcohol workers Housing officers and accommodation support workers Job Centre Plus advisers Child Support Agency workers
Youth	Parenting practitioners Adult social care workers Supporting People teams Drug and alcohol workers Housing officers and accommodation support workers Job Centre Plus advisers Child Support Agency workers	
Justice and crime	Youth offending teams Staff and managers of: • Youth Offending Institutions • Secure Training Centres • Secure Children's Homes Police in school liaison/child protection roles	Probation officers Multi-agency public protection teams Policing and law enforcement Prosecution services Custodial care
Sport and culture	Sports coaches and officials School and FE sport co-ordinators County sports development officers Sport competition managers School library service	Health and fitness providers Outdoor education/recreation providers Workers in cultural heritage, museums and galleries Performers in visual and literary arts Teachers of music and performing arts Library staff

Adapted from DCSF (2008e)

As you can see, the children's workforce consists of both a 'core and wider workforce' DCSF (2008e, p10). The core children's workforce identifies all those whose primary role is to work directly with children and contribute to improving outcomes for them. The wider children's workforce identifies those who may not necessarily work directly with children and young people as part of their primary role, but their role contributes to improving outcomes for children and young people.

CASE STUDY 1

Gemma is an early years practitioner working in the nursery class in a primary school. Gemma, along with the nursery teacher, provides activities to promote learning and development in children aged 3–5 years in line with the Early Years Foundation Stage Framework. The activities provide opportunities to enable children to make progress towards the milestones identified in the Foundation Stage Profiles. Gemma and the nursery teacher are directly responsible for improving outcomes for the children in their care; they are therefore part of the core children's workforce.

CASE STUDY 2

Steven is a Parent Support Adviser (PSA) working in a primary school. His role is to support parents to improve their parenting skills, to help them access the correct services they need or to give them the confidence to be able to support their child's learning and development. Steven's role is very diverse: he primarily works with parents, although occasionally he will work with the whole family. Rarely does he work with individual children in the absence of their parents. As a PSA Steven contributes towards improving outcomes for children, young people and their families; he is therefore part of the wider children's workforce.

If when embarking upon your early childhood studies degree you are not quite sure of the route you would like to take, it is worth noting that early years practitioners can be employed in a range of different settings, for example: nursery classes within a maintained primary school, private day nurseries, museums, libraries or working as part of a team of specialists working within Children's Centres, e.g. delivering stay-and-play sessions or working alongside health visitors. The opportunities available to you are endless.

ACTIVITY 2

If the 'children's workforce' involves all those who work with children, young people and their families, who do you think we refer to when we say 'the early years workforce'?

Much of the literature published recently (DfE, 2010, 2012b; DfE and DoH, 2011) refers to children in their 'foundation years', that is children from birth to five years of age, therefore we could assume that the early years workforce refers to those who work with children within this age group.

ACTIVITY 3

Think about the Jesuit motto, 'Give me the child until he is seven, and I will give you the man.' What do you think this motto suggests?

The motto in Activity 3 implies that everything a child experiences during the first seven years of life has a profound effect on their future life. This does not mean that anything a child experiences beyond the age of seven years will not affect their life; rather the motto suggests that the early years extend beyond the age of five. Indeed most early years courses, for example the Diploma in Childcare and Education, focus on children from birth to eight years of age. Therefore for the purpose of this chapter the early years workforce refers to all those who work with children from birth to eight years of age.

The early years workforce: policy and context

The publication of *Every Child Matters: Change for Children* (DfES, 2004a) highlighted the need for radical change in the way that services for children, young people and their families were to be delivered. DfES (2004a) advocated a more integrated approach to the way in which professionals from children's services worked together. In addition, DfES (2004a) introduced the notion of 'One Children's Workforce' wherein all those who worked with children, young people and their families shared the same vision and had the correct skills and knowledge to enable them to provide high-quality services. This vision continues to be a priority for the current Coalition government. DfE and DoH (2011, p59) states

> *Whatever their specialism, practitioners in the foundation years have a common commitment to children's healthy growth and development and working with their families. Making this goal a reality requires motivated, qualified, and confident leaders and professionals across health, early years and social care committed to working closely together in the interests of children and families.*

With regard to the early years workforce, since 1997 the government has prioritised financial investment in early years and childcare in order to increase the availability and quality of early years provision and to enable greater choice for parents. This included financial provision to improve the skills and knowledge of the early years workforce. Every Child Matters (ECM) (DfES, 2004a) provided the rationale for further investment in the children's workforce. The primary aim of ECM is to improve outcomes for young children and their families. It is widely acknowledged that this will be achieved through the development of a 'world-class workforce' which is competent and confident in meeting the needs of young children and their families, (DfES, 2004a). The Ten-Year Childcare Strategy (DfES, 2004b) set out to radically reform the early years and childcare sector, to ensure that childcare services in England were 'among the best in the world'. More recently, the government has made a commitment to continue to support young children in their early years stating that

> *All young children whatever their background or current circumstances, deserve the best possible start in life and must be given the opportunity to fulfil their potential.*

(DfE and DoH, 2011, p2)

The provision of a highly qualified and well skilled workforce is paramount if this vision is to be realised. As an early years practitioner you too will play a vital role in helping this vision became a reality.

We have talked about Every Child Matters (DfES, 2004a), acknowledging the influence that this policy has had upon the development of the children's workforce. However, since the Coalition government came into power in 2010, less emphasis has been placed on ECM. While the statutes arising from ECM remain (Children Act 2004 and Childcare Act 2006), current political thinking suggests that the terminology of ECM will change to reflect children's achievements, insofar as 'every child will achieve more'. Nonetheless, ECM remains one of the most important policy developments to date effecting the early years and childcare sector.

We might ask ourselves why has there been so much investment in developing the children's workforce, especially the early years workforce?

ACTIVITY 4

Begin to consider early years practice. Why do you think it is important to invest in the development of a highly skilled and well qualified early years workforce?

Research has proven many times that the qualifications and skills of early years practitioners are a major contributory factor in determining the quality within early years and childcare provision. Munton et al. (2002) suggest that staff qualifications are one of the factors which have a positive impact on improving outcomes for children. Practitioners who are well qualified better understand the importance of promoting early years environments which provide opportunities to promote child development. The Effective Provision of Pre-school Education (EPPE) research (Sylva et al., 2004) has played a major role in influencing policy developments with regard to the development of the early years workforce. Sylva et al. argue that the quality within early years provision correlates with the quality of the workforce, particularly in relation to the level of qualifications held by staff. More recently, Nutbrown (2012) acknowledges the influence that staff qualifications have upon the quality of early years provision and recommends that the government continues to invest in the professional development of early years practitioners, particularly the development of graduates with an early years specialism. However, qualifications alone do not ensure good quality early years provision. Fukkink and Lont (2007) highlighted that both informal and formal education and training contributed to the quality of early years and childcare provision.

Therefore, once qualified it is equally important that as an early years practitioner you engage in additional continuous professional development to ensure that your skills and knowledge reflect current thinking, both in terms of policy developments and curriculum changes.

Professionalisation of the early years workforce

For decades, the early years practitioner was always viewed as 'less professional' than others working in the area. Taggart (2011) argues that the general perception of the early years workforce was that it was solely concerned with the 'care' of young children rather than their education, and by virtue of this was perceived as 'less professional' than other caring professionals such as nurses. DfE and DoH (2011) also acknowledge the disparity between the professional status of those working within the early years workforce, insofar as some teachers viewed the early years practitioner less favourably than their 'teaching' peers, a view further supported in Simpson (2010, p10). The perception that the early years workforce was 'less professional' was perpetuated by the lack of a clear career structure and low rates of pay in comparison to other professions. However, when the Labour Party came to power in 1997, a concerted effort was made to radically reform the children's workforce, including the early years workforce, to enable the government's vision to have a 'world-class workforce' to be realised. The Ten-Year Childcare Strategy (DfES, 2004b) outlined the government's aspiration to have a graduate leading early years practice in every children's centre by 2010 and in all full day-care settings by 2015. The drive to professionalise the early years workforce in England is not only a means to improve quality, it can also be seen as an attempt to bring early years qualifications in line with those required by early years practitioners in European countries such as Sweden, Spain and also in New Zealand. Alakeson (2004, p23) states 'by 2012 it is expected that, early years and childcare provision in New Zealand will be led entirely by graduates, whereas in England by 2020 only 60 per cent of the early years workforce should be qualified to graduate level'. In the 2010 survey of early years and childcare providers (DfE, 2010a) it is reported that only 8 per cent of early years practitioners employed in full day-care were qualified to degree level, although the percentage of practitioners employed in full day-care in children's centres was higher at 19 per cent. The highest percentage of early years practitioners qualified to degree level was in maintained nursery schools and nursery classes. This is not surprising given that it is a statutory requirement to have qualified teachers leading early years provision in schools. In 2006, 80 per cent of primary caregivers of children aged 0–5 years in New Zealand were qualified to degree level (Statistics New Zealand, 2006). The percentage of early years practitioners qualified to degree level in England is low in comparison to the percentage in New Zealand.

In 2007 the government introduced a new professional status to give professional recognition to early years practitioners. The Early Years Professional Status (EYPS) provides a clear career structure for early years practitioners and is awarded to graduates who have demonstrated that they can lead and provide high-quality care and education for children from birth to five years. To be awarded EYPS, graduate early years practitioners had to demonstrate that they were confident and competent in all areas of practice as outlined in the EYPS National Standards. To date EYPS is the only professional status awarded to early years practitioners. However, Ranns et al. (2011) argues that the career aspirations of graduates achieving EYPS were seen as a threat to retaining early years practitioners within the private, voluntary and independent sectors, insofar as many expressed their intention to become a qualified teacher or take up a senior role within the local authority. In her review, Nutbrown (2012) recommends that an early years specialist route to qualified teacher status should be developed, suggesting that having teachers with an early years specialism will further raise the status of the early years sector and give additional professional recognition to early years practitioners. Introducing early years specialist qualified teacher status to the sector would enable further career progression for early years practitioners (see Figure 1.1) should they wish to gain qualified teacher status.

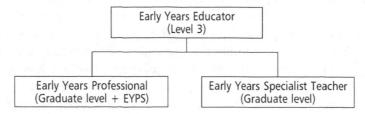

Figure 1.1 New career structure for early years practitioners
Adapted from DFE (2013)

ACTIVITY 5

Think about your own career aspirations and the options available to you. Has your original goal changed since commencing your early childhood studies degree? Consider the actions you must take in order to achieve your goal.

CASE STUDY 3

Sarah completed a level 3 qualification and gained employment as a teaching assistant working in the foundation stage of a primary school. While working at the school, she decided to study towards an early years sector-endorsed foundation degree as a first step to realising her ambition to become a qualified teacher. While studying on her foundation degree, the government introduced the Parent Support Adviser (PSA) initiative. Realising that she enjoyed working with parents and found establishing relationships with parents was one of her strengths, Sarah decided to change the focus of her career and was successful in her application to become a PSA working in a primary school. Since taking up employment as a PSA, Sarah has completed her level 4 Parenting Core Curriculum qualification.

CASE STUDY 3 *continued*

In recognition that at that time there was not a specific degree-level qualification relating to working with parents and families, the local authority worked in partnership with a local university to develop a degree in Applied Parenting and Family Studies. This was to ensure that practitioners working with parents and families were qualified to degree level, in line with the governments aspiration to have a graduate-led workforce. Sarah was successful in gaining a place on the programme. She continues to work as a PSA and has, for the time being, decided not to pursue her original goal of becoming a qualified teacher.

Diversity within the early years workforce

We have discussed the diversity of the children's workforce in relation to the various jobs roles. In this section we will discuss diversity within the early years workforce. Diversity is concerned with respecting and valuing differences between people, it is about encompassing all differences such as: age, race, religion, ethnicity, gender, disability and sexual orientation. The DfES (2005a) recognised the need for a diverse children's workforce which is able to meet the needs of children and their families from a diverse cultural, religious and ethnic background, arguing that the diversity of the workforce enhances children's experiences.

ACTIVITY 6

Reflecting upon your own childhood experience, think about all those professionals you came in contact with when at primary and secondary school. How many male teachers and how many teachers from black and minority ethnic (BME) backgrounds did you come into contact with? What do you think was the overall percentage of these in relation to all the teachers you met?

It is very likely that your reflections reveal that the highest percentage of professionals working in the schools and nurseries you attended were female and in most cases were white and British. Miller and Cable (2008) acknowledge that the early years workforce is a 'feminised' workforce, a view further supported by Rentzou and Ziga-nitidou (2009) who suggest that the early years workforce is 'gendered' with at least 85 per cent of the workforce being of the same sex, that is female. A recent survey of early years and childcare providers (DfE, 2010a) revealed that men represent between 1 and 2 per cent of the early years workforce, this is despite recruitment campaigns to try and increase the number of men employed in early years and childcare. However, the DfE (2012a) reports that there has been a 50 per cent increase in the number of men recruited into primary school teaching with the percentage of men working as teachers in primary schools at 19 per cent as opposed to between 1 and 2 per cent in the early years and childcare workforce.

ACTIVITY 7

Begin to consider early years practice. Why do you think that there is such a low percentage of men working in early years and childcare? How do you think that we could attract more men into the sector?

There are several factors which hinder the recruitment of men into the early years workforce, particularly in the private, voluntary and independent sectors. Rentzou and Ziganitidou (2009) suggest that there are many 'myths' concerning the reasons why men are reluctant to work in the early years workforce. One of these 'myths' is the apparent low wages afforded to early years practitioners compared to other professionals in the children's workforce. If we consider the case study below, we could argue that the low salaries afforded to practitioners employed in the private, voluntary and independent sectors are not a 'myth' but a reality that can deter men from entering the early years workforce.

CASE STUDY 4

Mark began his career as a nursery assistant in a private day nursery. He is now a room supervisor and his aspiration is to become a qualified teacher in early years.

> *I have always enjoyed being with young children and often look after my niece and nephew. I was always fascinated by how quickly they learnt new things; this fascination fuelled my desire to work with children.*

Mark is the only male member of staff employed at the nursery. When asked how the children react to this Mark says:

> *It is great being the only male member of the staff; the children gravitate to me, running up to me saying, 'Hiya, Mark'. Although I am aware that when new parents come into the setting they do give me a quizzical look, but once they get to know me they are great, I only wish more men would join the profession.*

Mark has just completed the Foundation Degree in Early Years and is studying towards the top-up degree in children and early childhood with Early Years Professional Status. He hopes to go on to gain qualified teacher status because

> *as a teacher, I will get a higher salary for the work that I do, and that is important to me, especially as I would like to marry and have children. How can I support my family with the income I receive in the private sector?*

Sakellariou and Rentzou (2007) suggest that male early years practitioners are a vital element of the early years workforce as they bring a new dimension to early years practice which is essential in meeting the holistic needs of all children. Male practitioners can be positive role models for those children from lone parent families. The latest statistics concerning the number of lone parents with dependent children in the UK reveal an increase in the number of female lone parents with dependent children. In 2011, 92 per cent of lone parents with dependent children were female, compared to only 8 per cent of male lone parents with dependent children (National Office for

Statistics, 2012). Taking these statistics into account, along with the findings of Sakellariou and Rentzou (2007), it is essential that we have a gender-balanced early years workforce to ensure that the needs of all children are met. Hopefully, the government's efforts to professionalise the early years workforce will attract more men into the workforce and redress the current gender imbalance.

Let us now turn our attention to cultural diversity within the early years workforce. Dunnell (2007, p5) states that *children in England are more ethnically diverse than other age groups.*

If we are to deliver children's services which reflect the diversity of children within communities, it goes without saying that the children's workforce should also reflect the communities they serve. The Day Care Trust Report (2003, p196) states that

> the recruitment of staff from black and ethnic communities can aid mutual understanding and can dramatically improve delivery of culturally sensitive services.

The latest early years and childcare provider survey revealed that approximately 17 per cent of the early years workforce are from black and minority ethnic (BME) groups (DfE, 2010a); it seems reasonable therefore to assume that the current early years workforce does not reflect the diversity of the communities it serves.

ACTIVITY 8

Begin to consider early years practice. Why do you think it is important to have a diverse workforce?

In 2007, the Children's Workforce Development Council surveyed 100 people to establish what children and young people wanted from practitioners in the children's workforce. DCSF (2008b, p14) states that they want, among other things:

- *Workers who have been through the same experiences they have and are going through.*

- *All people who work with them to have an understanding of equal opportunities, children's rights, child protection, disability awareness and confidentiality.*

If children and young people want early years practitioners to be empathetic, this can only be achieved if practitioners fully understand the challenges faced by those who are culturally different from the indigenous population. A culturally diverse workforce will enable children, young people and their families to feel better supported, which in turn will help to establish effective partnerships between practitioners and families and thereby improve outcomes for children, young people and their families. Taking into account the current low percentage of practitioners from BME groups within the early years workforce more needs to be done to train and recruit from these underrepresented groups.

CASE STUDY 5

A university in the North East of England had a significant number of mature male BME students enrolled on doctoral programmes. These students and their families lived in university accommodation for the duration of their course. While in residence, the children of these families attended local nursery classes and schools. The local authority in partnership with the university initiated a project to encourage the mothers to become involved in their child's learning and give them the confidence to support their children in nursery and school. While the primary aim of the project was to give the women the confidence to support their children's learning at home and to become more involved in school life, the long-term view was to hopefully train and recruit some of the mothers into early years.

After consulting with the mothers, it was agreed that female representatives from the local college would hold a series of practical workshops in which the mothers would be given the opportunity to learn about the meaning of play and how to support their child's learning. The women could all speak English, although some better than others. Fatima could speak fluent English and she volunteered to support some of the other mothers, working alongside the tutors.

The workshops proved so successful that the women wanted to learn more and it was agreed that the LA would support the delivery of an 'Introductory Certificate in Working with Young Children'. After successfully completing the programme several of the women went on to achieve their level 2 certificates.

As the women progressed through the programme, they gained confidence and some started to volunteer to support their children and others in their classroom. Fatima states:

> Before starting on the project I had to convince my husband that this was something worthwhile to do and that it would benefit the children. It helped that the workshops were delivered here at the university. The programme has really given me the confidence to go into school and support my child and other similar children. It has also given me the opportunity to gain a qualification. I look forward to studying for my level 3 certificate.

Skills required to work in the children's workforce

Taking into consideration the findings within the research identified above, as an early years practitioner, in whatever field of practice you choose to work in, if you have the passion to contribute to improving the lives of young children and their families, it is *your* responsibility to ensure that you have the necessary skills and knowledge to enable you to be the best practitioner that you can. Therefore, given that the early years is a dynamic and ever-changing landscape, as an early years practitioner working within the children's workforce you must be committed to your own continuous professional development.

As stated previously, if the government's vision to have a 'world-class children's workforce' is to be realised, it is essential that we have a children's workforce which is highly skilled and well qualified to meet the needs of all children and their families. The Common Core of Skills and Knowledge (CCSK) (CWDC, 2010) sets out the basic skills and knowledge required by all those working with children, young people and their families. It identifies six areas of skills which practitioners need to acquire if they are to become effective in their professional practice. The six areas identified are:

- effective communication and engagement;
- child and young person's development;
- safeguarding and promoting the welfare of the child;
- supporting transitions;
- multi-agency working;
- information sharing.

Given that early years practice is dynamic and ever-changing, personal professional development should be based upon reflective practice and should be a cyclical process (see Figure 1.2) to ensure that practitioners are skilled and competent to rise to the challenges presented with the changes to practice. An example of recent change is the introduction of the revised Early Years Foundation Stage Guidance (DfE, 2012b). As early years practitioners, areas for continuous professional development (CPD) are usually identified through supervision and appraisal meetings with your line manager. These are then recorded on your personal development record or training plan.

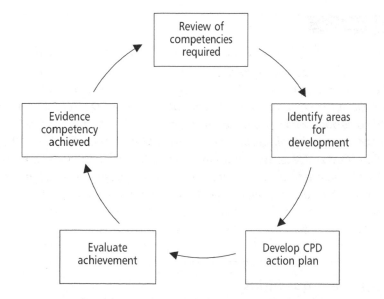

Figure 1.2 Continuous professional development (CPD) planning cycle

Whatever your role within the children's workforce you are required to demonstrate that you have the underpinning skills and knowledge to enable you to be a confident and competent practitioner. As you progress through this book you will be asked to identify those skills and knowledge which you need to develop your professional practice further. The training plan presented in Table 1.2 identifies the six areas of skills and knowledge outlined in the CCSK. Using the template below consider how you will acquire these skills and knowledge in practice.

Table 1.2 Personal development plan

Area of expertise	What do I need to learn?	How will this be achieved?	Resources required	Evidence of achievement	Target date
Effective communication					
Child and young person's development					
Safeguarding and promoting the welfare of the child					
Supporting transitions					
Multi-agency working					
Information sharing					

The responsibility for the development of qualifications and the continuous professional development of the early years workforce now lies with the Teaching Agency on behalf of the Department for Education (DfE) available at: **www.teachingagency recruitment.com/sections/about_the_org**.

CHAPTER SUMMARY

In this first chapter we have considered the term 'the children's workforce', acknowledging that it is used in reference to all those who work with children, young people and their families. We also emphasised that the early years workforce relates to all those who work with children from birth to eight years of age. From the research presented we have identified groups which are underrepresented in the children's workforce, namely men and black minority ethnic groups. Recruitment of representatives from these groups into the children's workforce, specifically into the early years workforce, is essential if the needs of all children are to be met. And finally, we recognised the value and importance of CPD to ensure that, as early years practitioners, we have the correct skills and knowledge to enable us to be confident and competent practitioners so we that can provide the best possible service to the children with whom we work.

Self-assessment questions
1. What is meant by the terms 'core' and 'wider' children's workforce?
2. What is greater, the percentage of male lone parents with dependent children or the percentage of female lone parents with dependent children?
3. Consider the case study of Fatima. What issues can you identify which may impact upon the recruitment of practitioners from BME groups into the early years workforce?

Department for Education (2012) *Early Years Foundation Stage Curriculum Guidance*. Nottingham: DfE Publications.

Department for Education and Skills (2004) *Every Child Matters: Change for Children*. Nottingham: DfES Publications.

Nutbrown, C (2012) *Review of Early Education and Care Qualifications: Interim Report*. Nottingham: DfE Publications.

2 Collaborative working within early years
Rose Envy

Reading through this chapter will help you to:

• reflect upon your own skills and the influence these have upon successful multi-agency working;

• critically appraise the concept of multi-agency working, relating this to good practice in early years settings;

• apply your understanding of the work in a multi-agency context to early years practice and identify areas for development to be included in your personal development action plan.

Introduction: defining collaborative working

The phrases 'multi-agency working' and 'collaborative working' just slip off the tongue, yet do we really know what we mean by these terms?

ACTIVITY 1

Before we begin to explore the notion of multi-agency working, think about all those professionals who work with young children and their families. Make a note of them.

Multi-agency working involves professionals from different agencies working together collaboratively to improve outcomes for children and their families. To aid our discussion, collaboration in this instance refers to a partnership of joint working between professionals from external agencies and early years practitioners. To improve outcomes for young children and their families, it is vital that they have access to the correct services at the time they are required; therefore we, as early years practitioners, cannot work in isolation from other services. Balloch and Taylor (2001) acknowledge the limitations of a single agency approach to solving social problems such as childhood obesity; therefore it is essential that we have an understanding of the services which are available to young children and their families. Services for young children and their families will include statutory services, voluntary services and private services.

ACTIVITY 2

In the previous activity you were asked to think about the different professionals involved in working with children and their families. Now, using the template presented in Figure 2.1, identify the different services that these professionals are located in.

ACTIVITY 2 continued

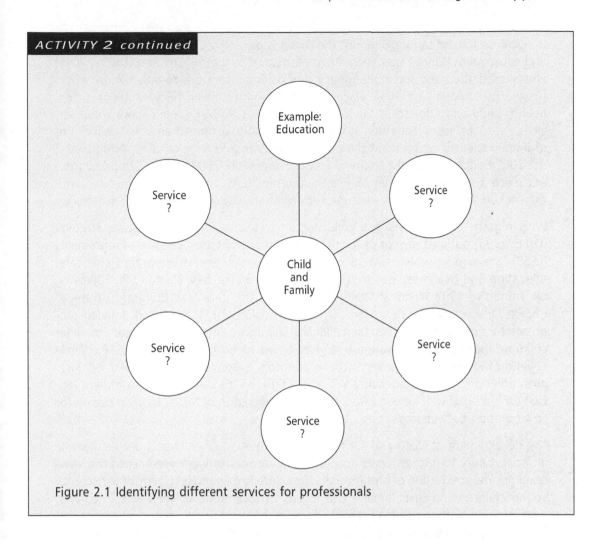

Figure 2.1 Identifying different services for professionals

Collaborative working: context and policy

To help us to understand and appreciate the importance of multi-agency working to improve outcomes for children and their families, let us remember the tragic death of Victoria Climbié in 2002. Victoria, and others before her (Maria Colwell in 1973, Jasmine Beckford and Tyra Henry in 1984, Kimberley Carlile in 1986, Leanne White in 1992 and Chelsea Brown in 1999), died at the hands of those who allegedly 'cared' for them. Victoria's death was seen to be the catalyst to improving multi-agency working between professionals. Lord Laming's report into the death of Victoria (Laming, 2003), identified, among other failings, that there was a systematic failure of communication between different staff and agencies which contributed to her death, and as a result Lord Laming recommended that professionals from the different services work more collaboratively and effectively together to try and prevent such tragic incidences from recurring. The Scottish Executive (2001, p27) states that *partnership working is crucial to the planning and delivery of integrated services.*

In response to Lord Laming's report, the Green Paper *Every Child Matters* (DfES, 2003) and subsequent White Paper *Every Child Matters: Change for Children* (DfES, 2004a) emphasised the need for multi-agency professionals to work together more effectively. The Children Act 2004 places a statutory duty on all relevant services, e.g. health, Child and Adolescent Mental Health Services (CAMHS), education, social services, etc., to work together through partnership arrangements to deliver co-ordinated services which meet the needs of children and their families. Additionally, the 2002 Education Act, the National Service Framework 2004 and the 2006 Childcare Act place a statutory duty on all local authorities (LAs) to work in partnership with external agencies to improve outcomes for children, young people and their families.

With regard to early years and childcare services, the National Childcare Strategy (DfEE, 1998) outlined proposals for the development of Local Sure Start Programmes (LSSP), the aim of which was to co-ordinate the delivery of integrated childcare, education and health services to give young children the best start in life. Following on from the 1998 National Childcare Strategy, the *Ten-Year Childcare Strategy: Choice for Parents. The Best Start for Children* (DfES, 2004b) outlined detailed proposals for improving choices for childcare and more integrated services for older children, including family support services based in both schools and LSSPs. While collaborative working appears to be a statutory responsibility bestowed on local authorities and external agencies, Williams (2009, p576) states that *government legislation is a significant step in establishing an expectation of rather than an option for collaboration between agencies*.

The development of LSSPs and subsequent development of children's centres provide an opportunity for professionals from different services to work together in the same building. The co-location of professionals from different agencies to provide services for young children and their families is a means of facilitating collaborative integrated working between professionals. However, we must not assume that just because services are co-located, effective collaborative working will automatically occur between those professionals. Blewett (2007) suggests that co-location alone will not overcome the challenges associated with collaborative working in a multi-agency context and argues that at a strategic level an explicit leadership strategy must be in place. It is worth noting that while at the time of writing there has been much discussion surrounding the recent closure of some children's centres, it could be argued that these centres closed because they were either not financially viable or perhaps the services provided through the centres were not meeting the needs of their communities rather than as a result of a lack of integrated working between professionals.

CASE STUDY 1

Coundon Children's Centre

The centre opened in 2006 and was developed from a Sure Start Local Programme. It is located within the Primary Care Trust building with a doctor's surgery, dental services, library and childcare provision in the same building. A multi-agency team which includes health visitors is co-located on site.

CASE STUDY 1 *continued*

Strong partnerships with parents and other services contribute to good outcomes for users. Very good communication and liaison with most partners provides highly effective support for users.

Staff and partners have a very clear understanding of their roles and responsibilities. High expectations, led by the example of the centre manager and senior staff, mean all the team are ambitious in raising aspiration and achievement. One parent said *they made me believe in myself and that my family could have a better life* (Ofsted, 2011a).

Challenges associated with collaborative working

The notion of collaborative working to deliver early years services appears to be a fairly straightforward concept; however, Greco and Sloper (2004) suggest that the simplicity of the idea is contrasted by the complexity of its implementation. Blewett (2007, p28) agrees with the view of Greco and Sloper and acknowledges the complexities and difficulties associated with collaborative working.

ACTIVITY 3

Why do you think that collaborative working is difficult to implement? List the reasons why you think this might be the case.

Effective communication

As we discussed earlier, one of the main findings identified in Lord Laming's report into the death of Victoria Climbié (Laming, 2003) was a lack of effective communication between professionals from different agencies. Lester et al. (2008) suggest that in order to function effectively and aid collaborative working all partners involved in the partnership arrangement must have the opportunity to meet regularly.

ACTIVITY 4

Begin to consider early years practice and think about those occasions when as early years practitioners we might meet with professionals from other agencies. How are these meetings arranged? How often are meetings convened? And what is the purpose of the meetings?

To be able to effectively communicate with professionals from external agencies we must first establish positive relationships with those professionals. Meeting regularly with professionals from other agencies is the first step on our journey to achieving this.

ACTIVITY 5

Consider the professionals and services you identified in the previous activities. To establish and maintain positive working relationships with those professionals consider the following questions:

- *How would you make contact and communicate in ways that are appropriate to the organisations and professionals?*

- *How would you present yourself and your own organisation in a positive light?*

- *How would you explain your role and the aims and objectives of your service?*

Effective communication between agencies was identified as a significant factor which facilitated effective collaboration between agencies working to deliver integrated services to improve outcomes for children and their families. Dawson (2007, p502) states that *effective communication between professionals is essential* and argues that *constructive interaction* between agencies is necessary to facilitate collaboration, particularly between professionals working collaboratively within the care sector – and this includes early years practice. Doyle (2008, p29) also acknowledges the value of effective communication between agencies and states that *teams can learn from each other about ways of improving communication*. For true integration of services to occur Edwards (2004) suggests that agencies must do more than merely work collaboratively, they must have in place an effective infrastructure to enable agencies to share systems and protocols which facilitate effective communication between professionals.

ACTIVITY 6

Discuss how as an early years practitioner you would promote the benefits of the Early Years Foundation Stage (EYFS) to other organisations and professionals. How would you:

- *Provide information on the benefits of EYFS which will be relevant to other organisations and professionals?*

- *Ensure the information is evidence-based and reflects good practice?*

- *Communicate this information in a way that is appropriate to organisations and professionals and their role?*

- *Persuade other professionals of the relevance of their work in encouraging children's learning and development?*

- *Deal effectively with queries and objections?*

- *Provide links to relevant networks and colleagues where appropriate?*

The EYFS will be discussed further in subsequent chapters.

Inter-agency trust

One of the most influential factors which impact upon the relationship between partner agencies is that of trust. The Audit Commission (1998) suggests that building trust between partners is the most important ingredient of success, therefore, for trust to be instilled in all stakeholders, effective partnership relationships must be fostered and maintained. McCulloch et al. (2004) also state in Glaister and Glaister (2005, p61) that trust is an important indicator in inter-professional collaboration; however, McCulloch et al. also suggest that trust is the result of existing friendship relationships rather than evolving from new inter-professional relationships. To establish trust between partners, all partners must have mutual respect and regard for each other's profession.

ACTIVITY 7

To establish trust between partner agencies, consider those professionals you identified earlier and think about:

- *How would you emphasise aspects of your work and the work of your organisation relevant to them?*

- *How would you check and improve the information you have about other agencies and professionals, their work and the people who their service is aimed at?*

Information sharing between agencies

Another significant factor which impacts on the effectiveness of multi-agency working is that of information sharing. Lord Laming (2003) identified that this was an area of weakness between agencies and subsequently recommended that multi-agencies should share information more effectively. Sharing information between agencies is crucial to the provision of early intervention and prevention services which meet the needs of children and their families. However, this is a very sensitive issue and does not mean that agencies should share all information with everyone all of the time. Professionals must exercise a degree of professional judgement when making decisions about sharing information with colleagues from other agencies. As an early years practitioner, you will need to be comfortable and confident in making professional judgements, therefore before sharing any information you must ensure that the information to be shared is accurate, based on facts and evidenced. Information should only be shared if it is in the best interest of the child and family, and in *most cases* consent must be gained prior to the information being shared. Where a child is at risk of significant harm professionals can share information without prior parental consent – this will be discussed in more detail in Chapter 8. In 2006 the government developed Information Sharing Guidance for all managers and practitioners which was revised in 2008. This guidance document identifies 'seven golden rules' which practitioners should take into consideration when deciding whether information should be shared (see Table 2.1).

Table 2.1 The seven golden rules of information sharing

1	Remember that the Data Protection Act is not a barrier to sharing information but provides a framework to ensure that personal information about living persons is shared appropriately.
2	Be open and honest with the person (and/or their family where appropriate) from the outset about why, what, how and with whom information will or could be shared, and seek their agreement unless it is unsafe or inappropriate to do so.
3	Seek advice if you are in any doubt, without disclosing the identity of the person where possible.
4	Share with consent where appropriate and, where possible, respect the wishes of those who do not consent to share confidential information. You may still share information without consent if, in your judgement, that lack of consent can be overridden in the public interest. You will need to base your judgement on the facts of the case.
5	Consider safety and well-being. Base your information sharing decisions on considerations of the safety and well-being of the person and others who may be affected by their actions.
6	Necessary, proportionate, relevant, accurate, timely and secure: ensure that the information you share is necessary for the purpose for which you are sharing it, is shared only with those people who need to have it, is accurate and up-to-date, is shared in a timely fashion and is shared securely.
7	Keep a record of your decision and the reasons for it – whether it is to share information or not. If you decide to share, then record what you have shared, with whom and for what purpose.

Adapted from HM Government (2008, p11)

ACTIVITY 8

Begin to consider early years practice. As a practitioner working in a private day nursery, think about the type of information you will be required to share and with whom you will need to share this information in each of the following scenarios:

- *At key transition points of the child's time at nursery, e.g. moving up into a different room in the nursery and moving up into the reception class of the local school.*
- *A child appears to have speech and language difficulties.*
- *You have noticed a sudden change in a child's behaviour.*

CASE STUDY 2

Transition into reception class from nursery

Jayne: Key worker for Leilah

Leilah was leaving nursery at the end of August and moving into the reception class of the local primary school. Prior to Leilah leaving nursery, I collated all the information held on file during Leilah's stay in the pre-school room. This included:

- observations and assessment information to demonstrate Leilah's progression towards the Foundation Stage Profiles;

- information concerning Leilah's health and well-being, which included dietary requirements and any known allergies;

- details of her friendship group while at nursery;

- samples of Leilah's work.

This information was shared (after obtaining consent from Leilah's parents) with the both the reception class teacher and support assistant who would be teaching Leilah in September. To facilitate good working arrangements with the school and to ease the transition from nursery to school, the nursery invited Leilah's new teacher and support assistant to visit Leilah in nursery.

Shared sense of direction

While there are statutes (Education Act 2002, Children Act 2004, Childcare Act 2006) in place to promote collaborative working between agencies at both a strategic and operational level, these alone do not necessarily mean that all agencies will collaborate effectively. Arblaster et al. (1998) suggest that if effective partnership working is to take place all stakeholders should have an awareness of the needs, services or goals of other agencies within the partnership. In addition, all partners should develop a shared sense of direction. The Audit Commission (1998) acknowledges that the development of joint strategies and accompanying action plans can facilitate the development of a shared sense of direction. The Apprenticeship, Skills and Learning Act (HM Government, 2009) bestows a statutory responsibility on LAs to develop a Children and Young People's Plan in conjunction with other service providers. Joint action plans will outline the different roles and responsibilities of the agencies within a broader multi-agency context. Within the context of early years practice, joint action plans at an operational level will include individual education plans (IEP) which outline the roles and responsibilities of those involved with children who have special educational needs.

We have discussed some of the challenges faced by professionals when trying to work collaboratively with other agencies. A prevailing theme associated with each of the challenges discussed is effective communication, without which we would not be able to share information, establish trust or agree a shared sense of direction. While as early years practitioners we may not be aware of the specific goals and targets of those agencies we work with and vice versa, we all share one commonality and that is we are all working together to improve outcomes for children and their families, and therefore this is the starting point for entering into collaborative inter-agency working.

Collaborative working practices within early years

In our initial discussion we explored the notion of collaborative working and acknowledged that as early years practitioners we can no longer work in isolation and that we must proactively engage with professionals from other agencies to ensure that children and their families receive the services they require at the time when they are needed. The focus of our next discussion will be to explore multi-agency working practices with in an early years context.

The Common Assessment Framework

The Common Assessment Framework (CAF) is a tool to facilitate integrated working between professionals from multi-agencies. It offers a standardised approach to the assessment and early identification of the needs of children and young people. The CAF is one aspect of integrated working arising from the Children Act 2004. While the CAF guidance (CWDC, 2009) is non-statutory, all LAs must give due consideration to it. If an LA deviates from the CWDC (2009) practice guidance they must ensure that they have in place an equally effective system for the early identification of children and young people's additional needs and the co-ordination of services to meet those needs.

As an early years practitioner you may be involved in the CAF process, either directly or indirectly. If you are a key worker for a child who requires a common assessment, you may be asked by the nursery manager to undertake the initial pre-assessment. Similarly, as a key worker you may be asked to attend the Team Around the Child (TAC) meetings to provide additional information to support the child and family. However, given that the CAF is a voluntary assessment, the child, parent or carer must give their consent prior to undertaking the assessment process. All early years practitioners who will be involved in undertaking a CAF must have received CAF training via their LA. Attendance at CAF training will be discussed and agreed by the nursery manager or line manager.

CASE STUDY 3

Initiating a CAF within an early years setting

Chloe is four years old and attends nursery to receive her entitlement of 15 hours of free early education. She attends nursery every morning from 9 a.m. until 12 p.m. Chloe is normally a very bubbly, bright and confident little girl who lives with her mum (Angela) who is a single parent and her ten-year-old brother.

Cause for concern

Over a period of five days Chloe's behaviour began to change dramatically. First, she began to look very tired and began to become withdrawn and tearful at the slightest thing. Jayne the nursery practitioner discussed her concerns with the nursery manager, who suggested that she should try to discuss her initial concerns with Chloe's mum.

Jayne was able to speak to Angela and it transpired that Chloe's father had stopped paying his child support payments and as a result Angela had found it increasingly difficult to manage her finances. Angela said she was very depressed and as a result she was very lethargic and short tempered with the children and the children's normal routine was not being followed, resulting in late nights for both Chloe and her brother.

Initiating the CAF process

Once Angela had overcome her initial embarrassment at the state of her financial affairs and the effect that these were having upon both her and the children, Angela agreed to being involved in the completion of a CAF. Jayne had attended the LA training so was able to carry out a CAF, and was asked to undertake the CAF because she had gained Angela's trust and confidence.

Jayne recalls that on the first occasion she was asked to complete a CAF with a family she was very nervous because she wanted to ensure that she obtained the correct information in a very sensitive way.

> *I am always acutely aware of the sensitivities faced by both parents and practitioners when completing a CAF. It is always difficult for families to admit that they need help, therefore as practitioners we have to act with tact and diplomacy and be completely non-judgemental.*

The lead professional

Another mechanism to facilitate integrated working practices is the provision of a lead professional (LP) who is the practitioner who takes a 'lead role' to make sure that front-line services are co-ordinated, coherent and achieving the intended outcomes. The lead professional role is intended to improve the co-ordination of multi-agency activity after a common assessment has been carried out. The role should reduce families' experience of repeated lengthy meetings, conflicting or confusing advice and uncertainty about who to approach for information. Technically, any practitioner can be nominated as the LP, and families can often request who they would like to be their main point of contact.

The term 'lead professional' should not be viewed as a job title; rather it is a set of functions to be carried out as part of the delivery of effective integrated support and as such should not be considered as a new role. In many cases practitioners are already delivering the three core functions:

- acting as a single point of contact for the child or family;
- co-ordinating the delivery of the actions agreed;
- reducing overlap and inconsistency in the services received.

A lead professional is accountable to their employing agency for delivering the lead professional functions. They are not responsible or accountable for the actions of other professionals from different agencies (CWDC, 2009).

Team around the child

The team around the child (TAC) facilitates multi-agency working by providing an opportunity for all those professionals involved with the child and family to come together, for example health, Child and Adolescent Mental Health Services (CAMHS), education, social services, etc.

The aim of the TAC is to:

- agree the needs of the child and family;
- support the child to meet their identified needs;
- arrange, as necessary, additional support based on a common assessment, as a pathway to targeted and specialist services;
- review the support given to the child and family;
- report, as required, to other review meetings or resource panels;
- identify gaps and inform planning and commissioning.

Adapted from CWDC (2009)

ACTIVITY 9

Begin to consider early years practice. To facilitate multi-agency working discuss how you would:

- *work to the goals and objectives you have agreed at the TAC;*

- *keep other organisations and professionals informed of your own progress;*

- *monitor and review the progress they are making;*

- *work with other organisations and professionals to evaluate the impact of working together;*

- *maintain effective working relationships with other and professionals throughout joint working.*

Models of multi-agency working

There are several models of multi-agency working which when explored can aid our understanding of the reasons why collaborative working is essential to ensure the effective delivery of early years services which meet the needs of young children and their families.

The service model of partnership working

The service model of partnership working as described by Arblaster et al. (1998) is premised upon the principle that collaboration is organised around systems that are convenient for the collaborating agencies at a strategic, locality and client level. With reference to these three different levels, at a strategic level we mean at a local authority level, that is senior managers within Children's Services or other services providing services for children and families, e.g. health or CAMHS. When discussing a locality level we are referring to geographical boundaries such as children's centre clusters. And finally, when referring to client level we mean all those children, young people and families who use the different services.

When applied to the delivery of early years services through children's centres, systems which are developed at a strategic level include the development of Children's Trust arrangements and the development of a joint strategy, namely the Children and Young People's Plan, which sets out how the LA intends to provide and improve its services. However, the introduction of the Health and Social Care Bill (DoH, 2011) has seen a shift in focus from CTs to the development of Health and Well-being Boards which will take responsibility for promoting integrated working practices at a strategic level. At a locality level, the Local Children's Boards provide access to specialist and targeted services. Collaboration at a client level occurs through client groups such as the parent focus groups within children's centres, the views of parents and other clients feeding into the children's centre management board. Lord Laming (2003) identified that information sharing was an area of weakness between agencies and subsequently recommended that multi-agencies should share information more effectively. This can only be done when agencies have in place the correct systems and protocols.

The systemic medical model of partnership working

More recently, within the systemic medical model (SMM) as described in Todd (2007) services are delivered around the child or family rather than through professional agencies. The SMM of partnership working is premised upon the assumption that all problems are inherent to the individual rather than to some extent being the result of external influences such as poverty and the interaction between the individual and the social context. Todd (2007) suggests that the SMM is premised upon the assumption that it is the 'child or family' which needs fixing, therefore there is little scope for families to be involved in the decision-making process. This model of partnership working does not support integrated multi-agency working as it could be argued that it is the professionals from a single agency who decide upon the services which are required. In relation to early years services, the SMM of partnership does not support the implementation of the CAF. Throughout the CAF process, professionals collaborate to agree the needs of children and their families, and the views of children and parents are also taken into consideration when commissioning services to meet their needs.

Collaborative model of partnership working

The third model of multi-agency working to be discussed is the collaborative model of partnership working as described by Smith et al. (2006) which is based upon the interaction between partners which encourages reflective practice. Within collaborative models of partnership working it is assumed that, in order to function successfully, all partners involved in the partnership arrangement (this includes parents and children where appropriate) must have the opportunity to meet regularly to aid collaborative working. This is in line with the recommendations made by Laming (2003). Within early years, an example of regular meetings where professionals come together to discuss the needs of children and their families is the Team Around the Child meetings.

ACTIVITY 10

To help you develop your critical thinking skills, consider the three models of multi-agency working discussed above. Think of one strength and one weakness associated with each model. Which model do you think fosters and maintains effective collaboration between all partners?

Food for thought. Do you think that different models of partnership working can be adopted in different scenarios?

The various models of partnership working discussed above attempt to provide an understanding of how effective collaborative working can be achieved. However, no one model provides a holistic explanation of partnership working within an early years context. There are elements within each model that contribute to our understanding of effective collaborative working. For example, the service model of partnership working emphasises the need for partnerships to have a supporting infrastructure in place which promotes effective communication between all partners. When discussing multi-agency working to improve outcomes for children and their families, Moran (2006) suggest that there is conflicting evidence concerning the impact that multi-agency working has upon improving outcomes, and draws the distinction between the impact that early intervention has upon improving outcomes and that of collaborative working. However, Allen (2011a) suggests that multi-agencies must work together effectively if children and their families are to benefit from early intervention, therefore as early years practitioners we must ensure that we proactively promote and facilitate collaborative working between those professionals with whom we work to ensure that all children receive the services they require at the time they are needed.

Skills required to facilitate collaborative working

The final section of this chapter will focus upon the skills required to facilitate effective collaborative working within early years. As stated previously, all those working with children and their families have a statutory responsibility to work in partnership with external agencies to improve outcomes for children, young people and their families. Therefore, it is our responsibility to ensure that we have the correct skills and knowledge to enable us to be confident practitioners. In his report into the death of Victoria Climbié, Laming (2003) stated that:

> There was a general lack of good practice between professionals working with Victoria which led to her death and that sometimes it needed nothing more than a manager doing their job by asking pertinent questions or taking the trouble to look in a case file. There can be no excuse for such sloppy and unprofessional performance.
>
> (Laming, 2003, p11)

The CCSK reflects a set of common values which underpin best practice which will facilitate effective multi-agency working by enabling multi-disciplinary teams to work together more effectively.

The skills identified by the CWDC (2010) for effective multi-agency working are:

Communication and teamwork

- Communicate effectively with own team and other professionals.
- Provide timely and succinct information to a range of professionals and parents.
- Record, summarise and share information.
- Competent use of ICT to share information.
- Work in a team context, internal and external to own profession.
- Develop skills and knowledge of other services.
- Share experiences.

Assertiveness

- Be proactive, initiate action, put forward own ideas.
- Persistence.
- Confidence.
- Present facts and judgements succinctly.

Adapted from CWDC (2010)

Using Table 2.2 identify those skills and knowledge which you need to develop further to ensure that you are a confident and competent practitioner.

Table 2.2 Personal development plan

Multi-agency working	What do I need to learn?	How will this be achieved?	Resources required	Evidence of achievement	Target date
Skills:					
Communication and teamwork					
Assertiveness					
Knowledge:					
You and your role					
How to make queries					
Procedures and working methods					

CHAPTER SUMMARY

In this chapter we have discussed the notion of collaborative working, stating that it refers to professionals from different agencies working collaboratively to improve outcomes for children, young people and their families. Throughout the discussion we have used the terms partnership working, collaborative working and multi-agency working interchangeably, because in essence it could be argued that they all mean the same thing. In this chapter we explored some of the challenges which are associated with effective multi-agency working and identified the skills required to help professionals overcome these challenges. Additionally, to aid our understanding of collaborative working we explored three contrasting models of partnership working, concluding that the most effective way to apply the various models to early year practices was to consider elements of each model, combining these to give a more holistic explanation of multi-agency working. Finally, we considered the skills and knowledge required to work effectively with other agencies.

Self-assessment questions
1. What are the three challenges associated with multi-agency working discussed?
2. Name the three models of partnership working discussed.
3. Identify a strength and weakness associated with each model of partnership working.

The first two chapters of this book have focused upon the wider issues associated with early years practice, both in terms of the wider children's workforce and working in the context of multi-agency working within children's services. The next three chapters will explore pedagogical practices within early years with a focus on a child-centred approach to children's learning.

There are many government guidance documents available to promote effective multi-agency working, all available from:
https://www.education.gov.uk/publications/standard/.../Page1/.../070.

Atkinson, M, Jones, M and Lamont, E (2007*) Multi-agency Working and Its Implications for Practice: A Review of Literature*. London: CFBT Publications.

House of Commons (2011) *Sure Start Children's Centres: Response to the Fifth Report from Children, Schools and Families Committee*. London: TSO.

Shibman, S (2007) *Children's Health, Our Future: A Review of Progress Against the National Service Framework, Young People and Maternity Services 2004*. London: TSO.

Together for Children (2009) *Facilitating Integrated Working Practices between Children's Services and Health*. London: TSO.

3 Developing child-centred practices
Rebecca Walters

Reading through this chapter will help you to:

- consider how a combination of historical and political issues impact on policy and practice in early years;

- reflect on your understanding of learning in the context of early years;

- begin to critically appraise the different types of play and how to support children in accessing them;

- identify areas for development to be included in your personal action plan.

Introduction: defining early years

Early years is a term that is widely used when talking about the care and education of young children, yet this is an imprecise definition (Bertram and Pascal, 2002, p5).

ACTIVITY 1

Before we begin to explore the notion of supporting learning in the early years think about the age range you consider it encompasses.

Most international research journals on early childhood focus on birth to eight years (Bertram and Pascal, 2002, p6) and for the purpose of this discussion we will adopt this definition. A clear understanding of why early years education takes the form it does today needs an understanding of the different perspectives that have dominated educational thinking throughout history as well as the shape of the contemporary curriculum:

> *History is a means of understanding (the) present states and challenges of early childhood education and is a tool for informing the shape of early childhood education in the future.*
>
> (Nutbrown et al., 2008, p4)

Historical influences on early years

Classical philosophical and theoretical perspectives considered early years to be a phase in its own right. Plato (478 BC) talked about the physical nature of young children and their need to run, skip and jump. He considered the difficulties young children have in sitting still and listening, advocating a practical play-based child-centred curriculum, moving to a more formal curriculum at the age of six. Much modern thinking about childhood and early education has been influenced by Enlightenment philosophers, notably John Locke (1632–1704) and Jean-Jacques Rousseau (1712–78), although they had quite different ideas about children, childhood and learning (see basic summary presented in Figure 3.1).

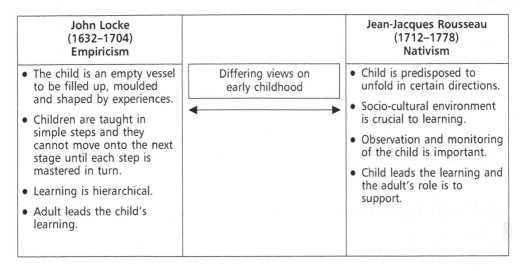

John Locke (1632–1704) Empiricism		Jean-Jacques Rousseau (1712–1778) Nativism
• The child is an empty vessel to be filled up, moulded and shaped by experiences. • Children are taught in simple steps and they cannot move onto the next stage until each step is mastered in turn. • Learning is hierarchical. • Adult leads the child's learning.	Differing views on early childhood ◄─────────────►	• Child is predisposed to unfold in certain directions. • Socio-cultural environment is crucial to learning. • Observation and monitoring of the child is important. • Child leads the learning and the adult's role is to support.

Figure 3.1 Different views of childhood, comparing Locke and Rousseau

---

ACTIVITY 2

Consider the different views of childhood held by Locke and Rousseau. What is your perspective about children and their learning? Do you think like Locke that the child is the empty vessel waiting to be filled? Or, as Rousseau suggested, are children predisposed to learn?

Organised provision for early education didn't begin until Robert Owen (1771–1853). A British social reformer, Owen was credited with opening the first educational setting for early years in the United Kingdom. He was not an educationalist but a mill owner and philanthropist in Scotland. Contrary to common practice at the time, he refused to have any children under the age of ten working in his mills and believed that education was the key to forming a civilised society. He provided a safe environment for children with a focus on a play-based curriculum so that parents could work in his mills. Once children could walk they were left at Owen's infant school, which focused on letting the children make their own choices through play. Owen did not equip the classes with toys as he believed that, when in groups, children should be able to develop their own games and activities from the natural environment. In good weather the children were based outdoors, moving indoors only when the weather was bad.

Many of Owen's ideas were based on the thinking of Johann Heinrich Pestalozzi (1746–1827) who recognised that young children were not simply little adults but in an important phase of development that needed skilled and trained teachers who recognised the need to educate young children differently to that of older children. Pestalozzi promoted the idea that children should learn through self-discovery in order to solve problems for themselves.

ACTIVITY 3

Many of the early influences around early years consider it a phase in its own right. They talk of the need for a child-centred curriculum.

What do you think they mean by this?

How do you think learning in the early years is developed?

Figure 3.2 gives a brief overview of other key educational thinkers whose legacies are still relevant today when thinking about early years pedagogy and the role of play.

Political influences on the context of early years

While these varying philosophical approaches to learning and the teaching of children are still relevant, educators also find that they have to deal with the practical politics of early years. Who decides the curriculum, where does the money come from and how do we assess children's learning, for example, are all questions that have had different answers provided by our society at different periods in our history. No practitioner can ignore these issues but understanding why they are as they are today again demands some historical knowledge.

The 1870 Elementary Education Act, covering England and Wales, was the first to make arrangements for provision of education for 5–13 year olds, to be supervised by local education boards. By 1905 school inspectors were ruling on rote learning and memorisation, the dominant teaching strategy used by these first schools, as inappropriate for children under the age of five. From this point onward children under the age of five were excluded from school.

While elementary education was being established as a responsibility of the modern state, during the late Victorian period and early twentieth-century provision of nursery education was neglected. The Plowden Report (1967) recognised this limited provision, highlighting the under-fives age range as *the only group for whom no extra educational provision had been made* (p291).

In 1972, following the recommendations from the Plowden Report, the Conservative government announced that by 1982 nursery education would be expanded to cover all three and four year olds. This remained an unfilled promise and nursery education was severely neglected throughout the 1970s and 1980s. Provision was uneven and dependent upon the different priorities of different local authorities.

It was not until 1996, following both the Rumbolt Report, *Starting with Quality* (1990) and Start Right (Ball, 1994) that the Conservative government introduced the first set

Rousseau (1712–78)

Rousseau believed that we are all born good, but we are corrupted by the evils of society. Through careful control of education we can work to control the 'perfect nature' of a child. He focused on the difference between children and adults with children developing through three stages. Different forms of education are appropriate for each stage. Education needs to be individualised for each child so they are nurtured and encouraged to declare free expression. Early education is based primarily on the senses and direct contact with the physical world.

Pestalozzi (1746–1827)

Pestalozzi focused on the individuality of children, promoting the idea that children learn through practice and observation. The teacher's role is to facilitate learning rather than to impart knowledge and education should be in tune with nature. Children learn through practical activity and should be free to pursue their own interests and draw their own conclusions. Observation of the whole child, focusing on the whole child, was crucial to supporting children's learning, along with a sympathetic approach from teachers. Pestalozzi saw education as the crucial factor in improving social conditions.

Froebel (1782–1852)

Froebel was interested in the early education of the child. He developed kindergartens for children aged 3–7. He highlighted the role of the teacher to guide and support children's learning. He used the term 'unfolding' of the child in relation to children's learning and he likened this to small flowers that are nurtured and cared for by the gardener. He highlighted the importance of language as a way of understanding concepts and play as the highest level of child development. He developed special materials that he called 'gifts', such as wooden blocks and balls of different colours and sizes that were used to develop a child's physical and cognitive development.

Owen (1771–1858)

Owen was appalled by the living conditions of working people, particularly the poor, so he set up a nursery to care for children whose parents worked in his factory. He believed nurture is the greatest importance in child development and developed an educational environment to support it. He promoted informal teaching that promoted first-hand sensory experiences. He believed that children's well-being was supported through caring teachers and he employed male and female teachers who had patience.

**McMillan Sisters
Rachel (1859–1917) and Margaret (1860–1931)**

The McMillan sisters were concerned with the health and education of children. They believed that for children to have a healthy mind they needed to have a healthy body. In 1911 they established an open-air nursery for young children. The children spent all day at the nursery and were provided with meals. The school focused on promoting the health of the children, ensuring they were well fed and clothed; in turn they believed their education was more effective. The physical needs of the children need to be nurtured to enable children to be educated. The children had large outdoor spaces to run and play in with caring as the central aspect of the curriculum.

Montessori (1870–1952)

Montessori believed that each child was an individual with a unique personality. Early education is about being child-centred, but not led by the child. The skilled adult is there to encourage the children to take control of their own learning and the carefully structured and arranged environment is considered the third teacher. The adult is there to observe and intervene when needed.

Figure 3.2 Key educational thinkers

35

of curriculum guidelines for pre-school settings, *Desirable Outcomes for Children's Learning on Entering Compulsory Education* (SCAA, 1996).

This was the beginning of increasing government intervention in early years. In 1997 'New' Labour came into power with the pledge that their priority, as Tony Blair, the party leader, put it, was to be: *Education, Education, Education*. They significantly increased the funding for the early years sector, pledging free nursery provision for all four year olds, as well as for three year olds whose parents wanted them in nursery education. They then revised the Desirable Learning Outcomes (DLO) as the Early Learning Goals (QCA, 2001).

This was followed by *Birth to Three Matters* (DfES, 2002), launched to provide guidance for practitioners working with children from birth to three.

Through the introduction of these frameworks there was a raised awareness of the importance of the early years of learning in a child's life with recognition of the need for a skilled workforce to support this phase. Labour introduced the Early Years Professional Status (EYPS) for practitioners working in the sector. Practitioners working in private day nurseries, Sure Start centres and childminders were given the opportunity to complete a degree and then progress through the EYPS where they had to demonstrate that they could initially meet 39 standards focused on work with children across the age range 0–5. In September 2012, this was reduced to eight standards, each with a number of supporting statements. The government made a commitment to make early years a graduate-led profession and set about promoting professionalism in the sector.

What does it mean to teach in the early years?

Government drives to produce a better qualified and higher status workforce led to the creation of Early Years Professional Status. The government guidance for the early years is certainly different in tone and approach to that for Key Stage 1 onwards and practice in early years is often seen as being based on different traditions and different conceptions of pedagogy. What does this mean for early years practitioners and how does it affect their role in the workplace? This has been the subject of substantial research in education in recent years and it would be useful at this point to reflect on how what you use in the role of an early years practitioner in a setting or school might be different to other educators.

ACTIVITY 4

Read some of the following journal articles by leading researchers in the field. Each of these research papers has a different way of positioning the early years professional and understanding how much control they have over their own practice. Then ask yourself the questions below.

Miller, L (2008) Developing professionalism within a regulatory framework in England: challenges and possibilities, *European Early Childhood Education Research Journal*, 16 (2): 255–68.

ACTIVITY 4 *continued*

Osgood, J (2009) Childcare workforce reform in England and 'The Early Years Professional': a critical discourse analysis, *Journal of Education Policy*, 24 (6): 733–51.

Simpson, D (2010) Being professional? Conceptualising Early Years professionalism in England, *European Early Childhood Education Research Journal*, 18 (1): 5–14.

- *Which of these would you say is closest to your own experience and why?*
- *How easy do you find it to step outside of government guidance in your practice?*
- *How easy is it for you to lead practice in your setting as EYPs are supposed to?*
- *What changes in working relationships might help you be more creative in your pedagogy?*

From the late 1990s, the early years sector was finally gaining recognition in terms of the provision of curriculum frameworks to support children's learning in this phase with the focus on using play as the medium for supporting children's learning. However, for practitioners working with young children, there was still a mismatch across the documentation, which differed according to the age ranges of the children (see Table 3.1).

Table 3.1 Age ranges of children in early years alongside the curriculum documentation (early 2000)

Age group	Curriculum guidance
0–3	Birth to Three Matters
3–5	Early Learning Goals
5 years onwards (Key Stage 1)	National Curriculum

In 2008 the Early Years Foundation Stage (EYFS) was introduced. Finally this document brought together all the phases from the previous documents, the Birth to Three matters framework, the Foundation Stage and the National Day Care Standards and collated them in one universal document to be used by practitioners in state or private settings working with children from 0 through to five years of age. This framework was based on the *overarching aim to help young children achieve the five Every Child Matters outcomes of staying safe, being healthy, enjoying and achieving, making a positive contribution and achieving economic well-being* (DCSF, 2008a, p7). The curriculum timeline presented in Figure 3.3 gives a brief overview of some of the curriculum frameworks introduced to support learning and development in the early years sector.

As you can see from Figure 3.3, from 1996 to the present, there have been several changes of curriculum guidance for the early years sector. With the introduction of curriculum guidance for the early years we begin to see the definition of early years as being the 0–5 age range. The revised EYFS (DfE, 2012b) is built around a practical play-based curriculum, with a focus on developing children's creativity through play-based

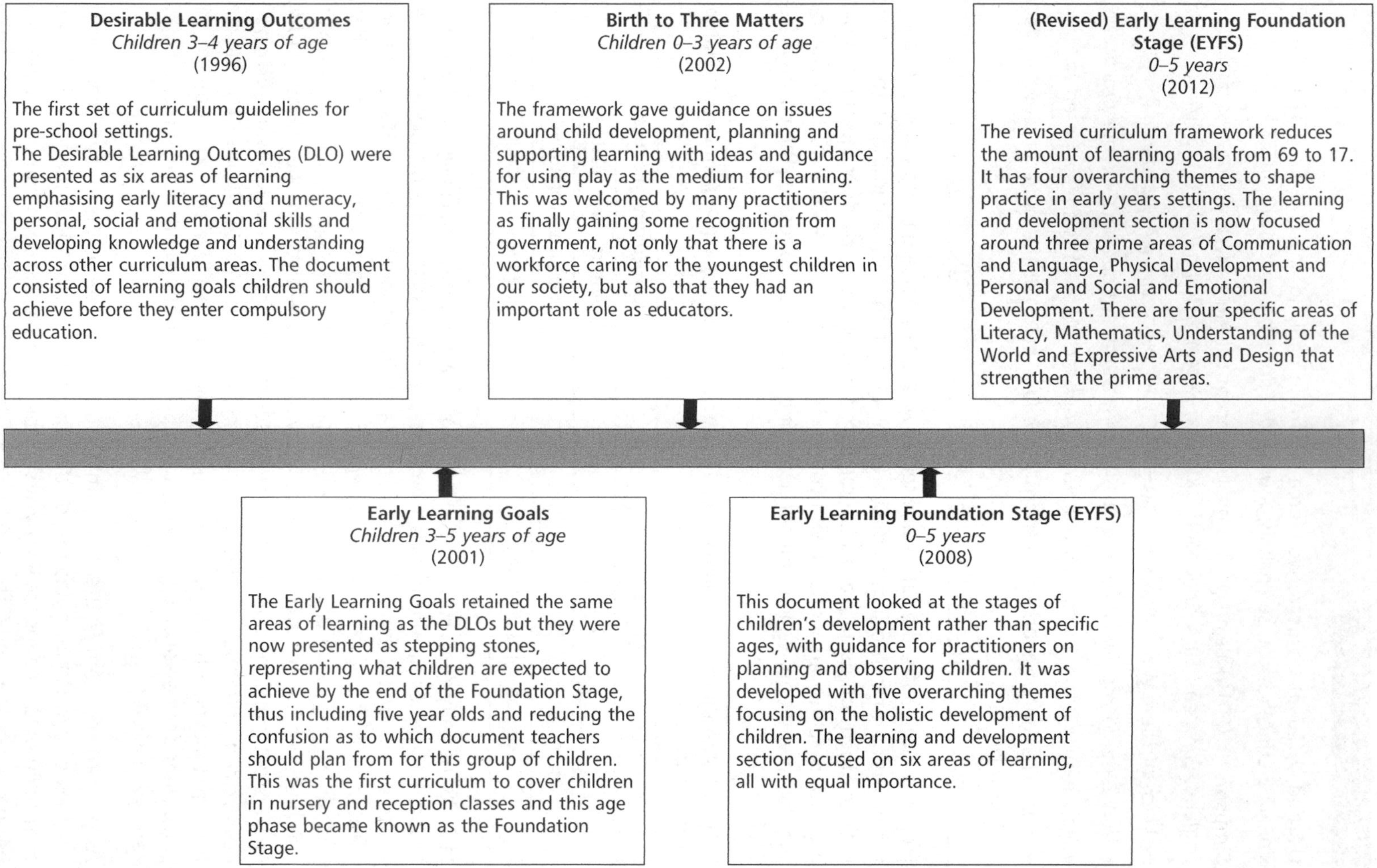

Desirable Learning Outcomes
Children 3–4 years of age
(1996)

The first set of curriculum guidelines for pre-school settings.
The Desirable Learning Outcomes (DLO) were presented as six areas of learning emphasising early literacy and numeracy, personal, social and emotional skills and developing knowledge and understanding across other curriculum areas. The document consisted of learning goals children should achieve before they enter compulsory education.

Birth to Three Matters
Children 0–3 years of age
(2002)

The framework gave guidance on issues around child development, planning and supporting learning with ideas and guidance for using play as the medium for learning. This was welcomed by many practitioners as finally gaining some recognition from government, not only that there is a workforce caring for the youngest children in our society, but also that they had an important role as educators.

(Revised) Early Learning Foundation Stage (EYFS)
0–5 years
(2012)

The revised curriculum framework reduces the amount of learning goals from 69 to 17. It has four overarching themes to shape practice in early years settings. The learning and development section is now focused around three prime areas of Communication and Language, Physical Development and Personal and Social and Emotional Development. There are four specific areas of Literacy, Mathematics, Understanding of the World and Expressive Arts and Design that strengthen the prime areas.

Early Learning Goals
Children 3–5 years of age
(2001)

The Early Learning Goals retained the same areas of learning as the DLOs but they were now presented as stepping stones, representing what children are expected to achieve by the end of the Foundation Stage, thus including five year olds and reducing the confusion as to which document teachers should plan from for this group of children. This was the first curriculum to cover children in nursery and reception classes and this age phase became known as the Foundation Stage.

Early Learning Foundation Stage (EYFS)
0–5 years
(2008)

This document looked at the stages of children's development rather than specific ages, with guidance for practitioners on planning and observing children. It was developed with five overarching themes focusing on the holistic development of children. The learning and development section focused on six areas of learning, all with equal importance.

Figure 3.3 Curriculum guidance for early years

exploration. At the end of the Foundation Stage the role of play is expected to shrink; in fact, the document notes *as children grow older and their development allows, it is expected that the balance will gradually shift towards more activities led by adults, to help children prepare for more formal learning, ready for year 1* (DfE, 2012b, p6).

In terms of pedagogy this creates a potential tension. What age should play cease to be important? Should we see childhood as separate and precious, like Rousseau and Montessori, or should this practical play-based exploratory approach be capped at the age of five?

Play

What is clearly a matter of consensus in educational thinking is that:

> *Play is, without a doubt, the most natural way children learn all over the world: this is why it is so important for us as educators, to ensure that children have every opportunity to engage in play and playful experiences.*
>
> (Moyles, 2010, p1)

This is visible in the more recent statutory guidance. The Early Years Foundation Stage (DfE, 2012b, p6) states that *children learn by leading their own play and by taking part in play that is guided by adults*. It suggests practitioners make a judgement with regard to the balance of play led by children and that led by adults. How though does it actually define play, and can play be defined anyway? These questions have been the subject of much debate in early years.

Our ideas of what play could encompass largely come from pioneers such as Froebel, Montessori and McMillan. All talked about the need for a play-based curriculum with the child at the centre, but in practice this is not such an easy task. Play is often interpreted differently by different practitioners (Canning, 2011, p8). There can be a tension between this 'idealised' or classic conception of play and actual practice in settings and although many teachers talk about play as supporting learning, play opportunities can often be limited and limiting (Wood and Attfield, 2005, p9). Our understanding of what the word 'play' constitutes across early years settings as well in the world of academia, as Moyles states, is not easy to pin down: *The act of trying to define play is difficult, as it is a multifaceted concept with many layers* (2005, p4).

In the twentieth century, as the new 'science' of psychology came to dominate educational thinking, the debate about play became enmeshed in newly emerging ideas of cognition.

Piaget (1896–1980) has been a huge influence on educational theory, in particular his ideas on the cognitive development of the child and their capacity to understand the world. His work was built on three basic assumptions:

- schemas;
- processes that enable learning to transit from one stage to another (assimilation and accommodation);
- stages of development.

He emphasised the importance of children's active engagement with the environment, focusing on how they make sense of their environment as they grow and develop and learn through a process of assimilation and accommodation. In this process awareness of the outside world is internalised as mental schemas, which then have to be adapted and changed to accommodate new information and experience.

Piaget described assimilation and accommodation as two different learning processes (see Table 3.2), but ones that coexist and take place simultaneously, as the child strives for 'equilibrium'.

Table 3.2 Assimilation and accommodation

Assimilation	Accommodation
The process of taking in some new knowledge from the environment so that they fit and mould with the existing concepts and ideas (schema). Existing ideas don't change they stay the same.	Old ideas are adapted and changes to accommodate new ideas and knowledge. Instead of assimilating them he reorders his understanding and change his viewpoint to accommodate the new information.
It's like having a mound of knowledge that just gets bigger and bigger as the knowledge is added to it.	In accommodation the mound of knowledge doesn't simply get bigger, it changes shape to accommodate the new information.
A child has an understanding that a horse is big, has four legs and a tail. The child sees a zebra for the first time and calls it a horse. The child has assimilated this information in the schema for a horse.	To accommodate the zebra, the child is told that it is not a horse but a zebra. A zebra is big, has four legs and a tail and it's stripy. The horse schema has been modified and a new schema has been created for zebras.

CASE STUDY 1

Aged three years and seven months, Matthew attended the nursery class in his local school five mornings a week. The nursery class had all of the usual play areas for young children, including water, sand, construction, home corner, arts and craft and design technology to name just a few.

The curriculum in the nursery followed a planning scheme that changed the topic on a weekly basis. For example, the overall theme for the half term may have been 'water', but each week the staff changed the focus to be more specific, such as, 'the sea' or 'the river'. As a result of this the resources in the water area were changed weekly to tie in with the planning focus.

In week one of the project the water area had jugs and pipes with connectors in. Matthew enjoyed filling and pouring with the jugs and watching the water flow down the pipes. He would become engrossed in this activity and spent some time each morning for the week playing with these resources. After the week ended, the focus of the planning was changed and the result was that the resources in the water area were taken away and replaced with different materials to reflect the weekly project focus. Matthew came

CASE STUDY **2** *continued*

into nursery this week and again spent time playing with the new resources that had been added to the water area. At the end of the week the resources were again changed.

Task
In terms of Piaget's schemas of assimilation and accommodation, what is the impact of the staff in the nursery replacing and constantly changing the resources in the water area? How could the staff encourage Matthew to develop his learning in the water area?

Piaget

Piaget saw schemas as fundamental to the learning processes of children. He also believed that all children went through four stages of development. These are loosely related to age and all children will pass through all the stages of development, in a fixed, universal order (see Figure 3.4).

Piaget viewed the child as leading their own learning, through interactions with the environment, with the child ideally making choices with as little adult intervention as possible. He promoted 'discovery learning', where children learn best through actively exploring and the adults' role is to facilitate this learning rather than overly direct it.

Piaget's theory rests on the assumption of children's readiness to learn new concepts or skills and on the notion that certain skills should only be taught when children have reached an appropriate stage of cognitive development and never before. He viewed the child as a 'lone scientist' and largely left unexplored the social context of learning and the use of language in children's development.

Although they are both constructivists, Piaget's ideas are often seen as opposed to the ideas of Vygotsky and his socio-cultural theory, which placed social interactions and language at the heart of its approach.

Vygotsky

Vygotsky (1896–1934) was a Russian psychologist engaged in research around the same time as Piaget. Vygotsky built his theory on the idea that the social and cultural aspects of a child's life are pivotal in their overall development, particularly in relation to cognitive development. He stated that every function of a child's cultural development appeared on two levels: first on a social level, between people (inter-psychological) and then on an individual level, inside the child (intra-psychological) (Vygotsky, 1978, p57). This leads to a conception of practice as being built around the child working with the more able adult to support them in an activity in the first instance and then developing the confidence and skill to attempt it independently. Vygotsky considered the more able educator to be someone who has a higher ability of knowledge or understanding of the particular task. This can refer to the teacher or another child.

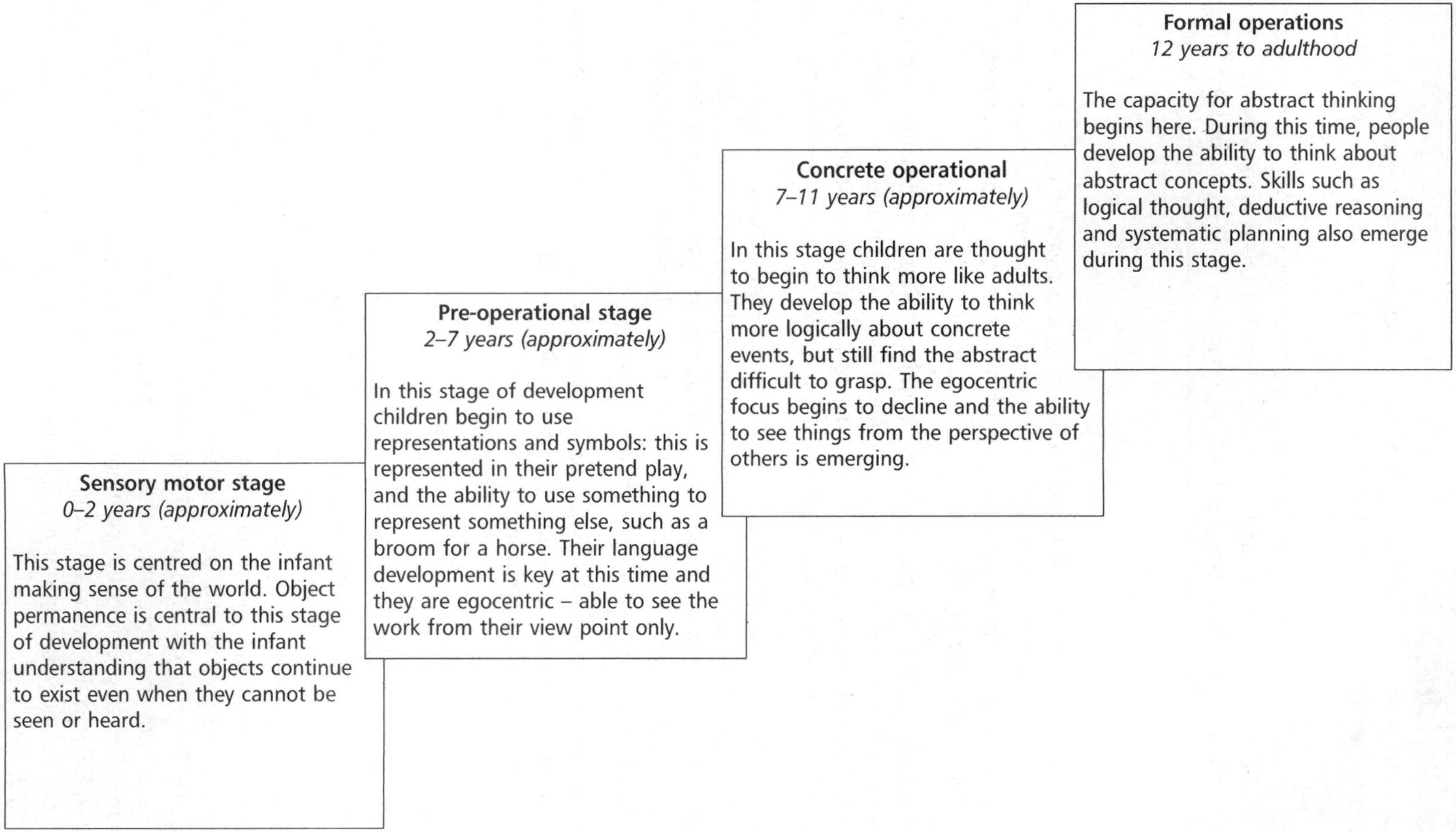

Formal operations
12 years to adulthood

The capacity for abstract thinking begins here. During this time, people develop the ability to think about abstract concepts. Skills such as logical thought, deductive reasoning and systematic planning also emerge during this stage.

Concrete operational
7–11 years (approximately)

In this stage children are thought to begin to think more like adults. They develop the ability to think more logically about concrete events, but still find the abstract difficult to grasp. The egocentric focus begins to decline and the ability to see things from the perspective of others is emerging.

Pre-operational stage
2–7 years (approximately)

In this stage of development children begin to use representations and symbols: this is represented in their pretend play, and the ability to use something to represent something else, such as a broom for a horse. Their language development is key at this time and they are egocentric – able to see the work from their view point only.

Sensory motor stage
0–2 years (approximately)

This stage is centred on the infant making sense of the world. Object permanence is central to this stage of development with the infant understanding that objects continue to exist even when they cannot be seen or heard.

Figure 3.4 Piaget's stages of development

This characterisation of the 'more knowledgeable other' is related to Vygotsky's concept of the Zone of Proximal Development:

the distance between the actual development level as determined by independent problem solving and the level of potential development as determined through problem solving under adult guidance, or in collaboration with more able peers.

(Vygotsky, 1978, p86)

We can think of the Zone of Proximal Development as a traffic-light system (see Table 3.3).

Table 3.3 Zone of Proximal Development represented as a traffic-light system

Green Learner can do independently	The things the child can achieve independently with no adult support	The three year old in nursery can put his coat on independently (he cannot yet fasten it up)
Amber Zone of Proximal Development	Areas of development relate to the activities the child can do with the support and guidance of the more able other	The three year old cannot fasten the zip on his coat. The more able other (*this could be an adult or a child who has mastered the skill of fastening zips) talks to the child while putting the zip together, encouraging the child to pull the zip up themselves
Red Learner cannot yet do	This is what the child will be able to do independently in the future	Following the guidance and scaffolding from the more able other, encouraging the child to try and put the zip together and pull it up themselves. Eventually, in the future the child will do this independently

The Zone of Proximal Development (amber section) is the optimum point for learning for a child. In early years this is the point where practitioners need to carefully plan activities matched to the child to take them beyond their current level of learning. This is the point where the child has some pre-existing knowledge that can be developed further through the support of the more knowledgeable other. Keeping planned activities in the green zone will not result in the development of learning and can lead to children disengaging because they are bored. Planning activities for children in the red zone, when they are not prepared for them, can result in activities the child is not yet capable of achieving and can cause children anxiety at the difficulty of the task. This creates a critical stage that practitioners need to carefully manage in the planning process:

Pedagogy had to be orientated not towards the yesterday of development but towards tomorrow and the only good teaching is that which outpaces development.

(Vygotsky, cited in Leach and Moon, 1999, p43)

ACTIVITY 5

Think about how Vygotsky's theory looks in practice and consider the case study above regarding Matthew and the water. How would Vygotsky's theory be used to develop and enhance his learning.

How does this sit in contrast with Piaget?

Although there are areas in the theories of Piaget and Vygotsky that are in contrast to each other, both agreed on certain aspects of child development and, in particular, on the role in this of play. Piaget (1929) talked about play serving many purposes and since, in his view, children learn more effectively through activity than instruction, play provides an excellent vehicle for learning.

In Vygotsky's view:

> *In play, a child is always above his average age, above his daily behaviour; in play, it is as though he were a head taller than himself. As in the focus of the magnifying glass, play contains all developmental tendencies in a condensed form and is itself a major source of development.*

> (Vygotsky, 1978, p102)

ACTIVITY 6

Brooker and Edwards (2010, p9) note that Piaget and Vygotsky have had a powerful impact on educational initiatives and curricula.

The Early Years Foundation Stage curriculum guidance states the need for planned, purposeful play that should be a mix of adult-led and child-initiated activity.

How can you see some of the ideas of Piaget and Vygotsky reflected in the above statement?

If we work from the classical conception of play, developed since Plato and the early years pioneers, it will enable us to look more closely at how we can manage play in the context of an early years curriculum. Play is difficult to pin down as so many things can be deemed to be play; the one thing academics and practitioners can agree on is that there is no common agreement to this question (Canning, 2011, p9)! However, many educationalists have nevertheless attempted to define play.

Parten (1932) identified four distinct stages that children go though in their play as they grow and develop. While all children are individual and develop at their own pace, most will progress through the four stages of play presented in Table 3.4.

Table 3.4 Four stages of play

Solitary play	The child plays on their own regardless of the activities that are going on around him/her.
Parallel play	As young children begin to become more aware of the environment and others around them, they begin to participate in parallel play in which they play alongside other children. They may be interacting with each other but not necessarily playing with each other.
Associative play	As children begin to develop more interest in their peers and other children they begin to engage in associative play when they begin to interact and may play together on the same activity.
Co-operative play	Play in which children will talk to each other and play on the same activity, discussing and working together to achieve a common goal.

Source: Parten (1932)

Common criteria of play

Krasnor and Pepler (1980) suggested four common criteria present in definitions of play:

- Intrinsic motivation – motivation from within to engage in the activity, not because someone has told you to do the activity.
- Flexibility – there is the opportunity to change the direction and focus of the behaviour. It is not rigid and can change over time and context.
- Positive effect – pleasure is gained from the activity.
- Non-literality – it does not follow a serious pattern or sequence, it has more of a pretend quality about it.

For Krasnor and Pepler (1980), the more criteria present simultaneously, the better the quality of play that is being engaged in. Rubin et al. (1983, p694) developed this further through considering that:

> *play is intrinsically motivated, concerned with means rather than ends, is child-directed, nonliteral, free from externally dictated rule structures, rules that do exist can be modified by players, and requires active engagement of players.*

ACTIVITY 7

If you consider Krasnor and Pepler's criteria for play consider the following activities:

- *Children playing a game of football. To play the game the children have to follow the rules and there is no flexibility to change or adapt these rules. The game follows a serious pattern and the players have to follow the rules. Some children will lose the game and this may not give them pleasure. Considering the play criteria listed above do you think these children are playing?*

ACTIVITY 7 continued

- *A child choosing to play with their dolls, dressing them and getting them ready to go on a pretend shopping trip. The child has chosen this activity themselves, there are no rules to the activity and the child is choosing the direction of the play. Consider the four criteria listed from Krasnor and Pepler do you think this is a better quality of play that the game of football described above?*

Now consider how Rubin et al. have developed the criteria further. Does this change or strengthen your ideas about the quality of the play?

CHAPTER SUMMARY

In this chapter we have considered some of the major influences that have impacted on early years. In order to develop an understanding of the curriculum and what it looks like today it is important to have some knowledge of where it has come from. This means looking at both historical and political influences. In the further chapters we will begin to consider the challenges for practitioners in implementing the statutory guidance and how the historical perspectives influence this. As Wood and Attfield (2005: 1) highlight, its place [play] in the curriculum remains problematic, particularly beyond the early years of school.

Self-assessment questions

1. Do you think that there is a tension between play and other aspects of the early years curriculum?
2. How would you begin to define play in its broadest sense?
3. Can you think of activities that you would define as:
   - playful;
   - making use of Piaget's theories;
   - making use of Vygotsky's theories?

FURTHER READING

Brooker, L and Edwards, S (2010) *Engaging Play*. Maidenhead: Open University Press.

Canning, N (2011) *Play and Practice in the Early Years Foundation Stage*. London: Sage.

House, R (ed.) (2011) *Too Much Too Soon: Early Learning and the Erosion of Childhood*. Gloucestershire: Hawthorn Press.

Neaum, S (2013) *Child Development for Early Years Students and Practitioners*. Exeter: Learning Matters.

Nutbrown, C, Clough, P and Selbie, P (2008) *Early Childhood Education: History, Philosophy and Experience*. London: Sage.

Wood, E (2007) Reconceptualising child-centred education: contemporary directions in policy, theory and practice in early childhood, *FORUM*, 49 (1 and 2): 119–35.

Wood, E and Attfield, J (2005) *Play, Learning and Early Childhood Curriculum*. London: Paul Chapman.

4   Pedagogy
Rebecca Walters

Reading through this chapter will help you to:

- critically reflect upon the range of personal experiences that have influenced your professional practice;

- critically analyse the relationship of early years practice to educational policies;

- critically reflect upon the impact of professionals on children's learning;

- identify areas for development to be included in your action plan.

What do we mean by pedagogy?

We start with the premise that teachers are naturally curious about pedagogy.

(Leach and Moon, 2008, p4)

This is an interesting starting point for this chapter as the term 'pedagogy' *does not enjoy widespread currency in England* (Alexander, 2004, p9). In fact, when opening my lectures on early childhood pedagogy at the start of term, the opening question in the lecture theatre is: 'Who knows what this word means?' Unsurprisingly very few, if any, hands go up. This is not just due to early term nerves at answering a question in front of a large lecture audience but more about the language of pedagogy being relatively unfamiliar to a wide range of practitioners, teachers and students in the field of education. Over twenty years ago the noted British educationalist Brian Simon (1985, p77) highlighted the stark contrast between England and other European countries, where *the term 'pedagogy' has an honoured place* and it appears this characterisation might still have some truth in it.

ACTIVITY 1

Consider the term 'pedagogy'.

- *What is your understanding of this word?*

- *How do you think pedagogy is relevant to your work in the early years sector?*

Make some notes to highlight your knowledge and understanding of this concept.

There are many definitions of the term pedagogy, the most commonly accepted one in England being: *the art, or science, of teaching*. Alexander (in Hall et al., 2008, p3) distinguishes pedagogy from teaching by considering teaching to be

> *an act, while pedagogy is both the act and discourse. Pedagogy encompasses the performance of teaching together with the theories, beliefs, policies and controversies that inform and shape it.*

Pedagogy, then, is more than just the act of teaching. Teaching is the final outcome of the pedagogical processes. These processes are formed by our

> *understanding of how children learn and develop, and the practices through which we can enhance that process. It is rooted in values and beliefs about what we want for children, and supported by knowledge, theory and experience.*

> (Stephen and Pugh, cited in DCSF, 2009a, p4)

All of these factors combine to shape the way you teach, communicate and collaborate with children to support their learning. Because people do not see these underpinning factors (and see only the outcomes in the way you present yourself i.e. the way you 'do' rather than the thinking and background knowledge and experiences that come beforehand), in a way our pedagogy is unseen. It is the invisible aspect of teaching.

It is also important to recognise that being an individual and being a teacher/practitioner are inextricably linked. Your individual experiences as a person influence who you will be as a teacher/practitioner.

My pedagogy: invisible influences on practice

We have discussed above the notion of pedagogy in its broadest sense. In this next section we will consider those experiences within our own lives that influence and impact upon us as practitioners. These experiences can be drawn from every aspect of our lives as I have tried to represent in Figure 4.1.

Some of the experiences you considered will have had a very positive impact upon who you are today; others may have had a negative influence on you as a practitioner. Negative experiences can have just as strong an effect as positive ones and can often turn us towards a search for ways of teaching we see as more productive or exciting than the ones we had to endure as children, or put into action as students, ourselves. Becoming aware of these influences, reflecting upon them and your own relationship to them is one way of starting to become aware of and self-consciously articulate your own pedagogy. If we don't reflect on this and make our own principles, beliefs and theories about education clear to ourselves we perhaps are doomed to repeat the mistakes we experienced, a past feature of English education systems noted as far back as 1912 when Edmund Holmes in his survey of elementary education noted that:

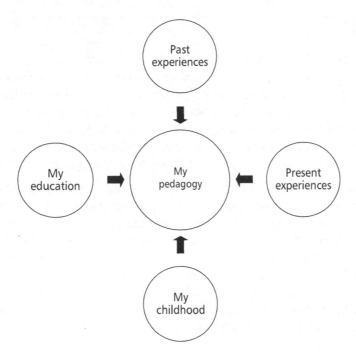

Figure 4.1 My pedagogy

Why is the teacher so ready to do everything (or nearly everything) for the children whom he professes to educate? One obvious answer to this question is that for a third of a century (1862–1895) the 'Education Department' did everything (or nearly everything) for him. For a third of a century 'My Lords' required their inspectors to examine every child in every elementary school in England on a syllabus which was binding on all schools alike. In doing this, they put a bit into the mouth of the teacher and drove him, at their pleasure, in this direction and that. And what they did to him they compelled him to do to the child.

(Holmes, 1912, p7)

Early school experiences and their impact on pedagogy

It is useful to look right back to your own early educational experiences and think about the potential impact of these on your own beliefs. Your own education is your earliest experience of teaching and, therefore, provides some of the earliest factors in the formation of your pedagogy. Look at the autobiographical account below high-lighting an educational experience/memory of my own and consider the impact this could have had on my personal pedagogy.

Autobiographical account 1

As a relatively confident six year old I remember going into Year 2 in primary school. It was very exciting going into this class as it signalled that I was one of the oldest children in what was then known as the infant school. We saw the school as relying on us older children to set an example to the younger ones, a challenge I relished. I remember the teacher vividly; she was a very short woman called Mrs Carnaby. However short she was, her voice and personality were huge and, at times, terrifying to a small child!

Mrs Carnaby was very keen on putting children 'on the spot' and asking you in front of the whole class to answer a maths question, usually a times table. I was not very good at my times tables. I found them really hard to remember and, sitting in her class, was regularly filled with dread at the thought that I would be the person she would pick on to answer the next question. I was usually a confident child, but in this class I would often sit trying not to look at her in case she picked me. The really frightening aspect of all this, being a six year old, was her response if you got the answer incorrect. She would humiliate us in front of the whole class, sometimes climbing onto her desk and hurling the blackboard rubber at the child who had 'got it wrong' before making them write out the sum to remember it.

Tasks
Think about this classroom experience. How do you think it will have impacted on me becoming a teacher? How would that experience re-enact itself in my pedagogy?
Think about that child, me. How do you think my experiences with this teacher impacted on my confidence and my attitude towards maths?

Autobiographical account 2

When I was in secondary school I took physics as a GCSE option. It was a decision I instantly regretted when I started the physics programme! I found it incredibly hard and struggled to understand the concepts we looked at. I was quite happy to give up and focus on my other subjects that I was enjoying. However, the physics teacher at the time was, thankfully, not willing to give up! Even though my performance was poor, he supported me through extra lessons, unpicking the concepts and taking the time to develop my confidence in the subject with a 'you are capable of this' approach, while developing my understanding of the subject. He patiently reframed the different concepts, laws and processes I had to follow to achieve at the subject until I could understand the task I was set. Put simply, he had faith in me that I could do it and this helped me to have faith in myself.

Task
How might this experience impact on my pedagogy? How do you think this may be re-enacted in my practice? How does this differ from autobiographical account 1?

ACTIVITY 2

Think back to your early school experiences: can you recall an incident, experiences or specific teachers that impacted on you and your learning? These experiences can be positive or negative. How do you think this is re-enacted in your practice with young children? Do you repeat some of these positive attitudes and practices or do you deliberately avoid some of the negative ones? Are there other practices that you have copied from early experience without particularly questioning them?

As practitioners working and supporting young children in their learning and development we hold a privileged position and our actions can stay with children for the rest of their lives. This can be quite overwhelming when you look back and consider the impact educators and others have had on you. Quite simply, *pedagogy can change people's lives. It has the power to transform* (Leach and Moon, 2008, p173).

Looking back on autobiographical account 1, I can see that the actions of Mrs Carnaby are still with me today and have impacted on me as a teacher working with young children. I entered year 2 as a confident six year old but when I left that class I was not as confident and had developed a concept of myself as someone who was 'not very good' at maths. This stayed with me throughout my primary years. As a teacher this formed part of my pedagogy in that I didn't put children on the spot, I was very reluctant to ask a child to answer a question if they didn't volunteer the information, and if I did I was sensitive in the way I asked them.

To be an effective early years practitioner we need to be mindful of those experiences which help to shape our practice, something now reflected in recent government guidance for the early years (DCSF, 2009a, p4) which noted that:

> *The more we are aware of our practices – what we do, why we do it, its impact on children and their learning – the more we reflect, learn and develop our practice the more effective we will be. This is developing our pedagogy.*

Pedagogy is not something that just appears, however, based on a handful of experiences and then remaining static. It is an evolving process. Different life experiences and continuous professional development develops and changes your pedagogy throughout your life as an educator.

CASE STUDY 3

Autobiographical account 3

My whole life changed following the birth of my first son Matthew. My approach to children and parents was challenged when this small bundle came into my life and rearranged all of my priorities and my lifestyle. Then, following the birth of my twin girls, Neve and Lois, my life was turned upside down again. This huge change in my personal life impacted significantly on my beliefs as a teacher. Having a young child at

CASE STUDY 3 *continued*

home made me much more sensitive to their needs with a developing first-hand experience and understanding of both how vulnerable they are and of how they are constantly learning from the moment of birth.

Motherhood particularly changed my attitude to the importance of parents as partners in their child's education and of the kind of support they need when their child is settling into school. I was much more aware of how hard the parent can often find dropping their child off at school and of the kind of support that teachers can offer to make it easier for them and the child, for example, because I had now experienced it for myself.

Task
Consider an aspect of your personal life. How this has changed you and your beliefs around education?

The theoretical underpinnings of our personal pedagogy

If we look back to Alexander's (2004) definition of pedagogy he considers that part of this are the theories we use. These inform our understanding of the purposes of education and are crucial in developing our personal pedagogy. *The Key Elements of Effective Practice* (DfES, 2005b, p6) highlighted the need for practitioners working in the early years to have an understanding of how children develop and learn, as well as subject knowledge of the curriculum areas.

Shulman (1987) refers to this as 'pedagogical content knowledge', that is a combination of our understanding of the subject content alongside the theoretical understanding of how children learn. He highlights the need to have awareness and knowledge of the elements of subject matter (or curriculum) while using an understanding of how children learn. This latter part comes from the theoretical perspectives we have on childhood, based partly on the classic, and sometimes more contemporary, theories of child development and learning we are taught in university and at college and through continuous professional development.

How do we begin to form our theories as to how children learn? We all have ideas and opinions about education, some implicit and some explicit. Many of these ideas are first developed in the context of our university/college training, when we first study how children learn and develop (see Chapter 3 on child-centred learning and Chapter 5 on enhancing practices in the early years).

Working with these theories can help us to interpret aspects of children's learning in ways helpful to us as educators, putting pedagogical problems into a framework that enables us to see a solution that can enhance the child's learning (see Case Study 4 below).

CASE STUDY 4

Autobiographical account 4

Prior to starting on my teacher training degree programme I engaged in a range of work experience placements across several settings. In one particular setting I was working in the toddler room, with children aged between one and a half and three years. I became fascinated with watching one of the children, Becky, who consistently walked around the room with a bag from the home corner. She would go around collecting objects from the different areas filling her shopping bag. I noticed that Becky seemed to engage in this activity regularly in the course of a day and over a series of days. Sometimes the bag changed and she would use a bucket to transport the materials. One day Becky started carrying the sand from the sand tray into the home corner and the teacher told her off. I thought nothing more about the strange behaviour until I started looking at the concept of schemas, introduced by Piaget and developed by Chris Athey. It was like a penny dropping when I realised that what the teacher had seen as strange behaviour from Becky was actually a transporting schema being followed.

Tasks

How did the development and understanding of knowledge add to my pedagogy and in turn become useful in my approach to teaching and learning?

With my new knowledge about schemas how could I have supported Becky in her development?

Instead of telling Becky off how could the teacher have supported this stage in Becky's development?

ACTIVITY 3

Write a few paragraphs summarising your views about teaching.
What would you call your personal 'philosophy of teaching'?

Schemas

Piaget first introduced us to schemas through his work, but this was further developed through the work of Chris Athey. Schemas are patterns of repeatable behaviour that can be noticed in children's play and can illustrate their combining of thinking and exploration (see Table 4.1). Because schemas follow interests children can develop high levels of concentration and learning through them. The schema is chosen by the child and can be explored in different situations. Some children show one particular schema particularly strongly while others show several at once. Understanding schemas are useful as it can help us to understand and support a child's thinking and enable us to work from the interests of the child.

Table 4.1 Schemas and possible behaviours

Schema	Possible behaviours
Transporting	A child may carry blocks in a bag from one place to another
	They may move the sand from the sand tray to the water tray
	A child may push their friend round in a trolley or pushchair
Rotation	A fascination with spinning washing machines
	Rolling down hills
	Spinning round or being spun round
	Painting in a large circular motion
	Playing with toys with wheels such as cars and trucks
Connection	Engaging in activities where parts have to be joined together such as a train track and construction activities
Transforming	Adding sand to the water tray and vice versa
	Adding colour
Trajectory	Bouncing and kicking balls
	Dropping things from the cot or high chair
	Climbing and jumping
	Lining up cars
Enveloping and containing	Covering themselves with blankets
	Wrapping dolls and toys up
	Covering their painting with one colour
	Filling and emptying containers
	Making dens

The benefits of a professional early years workforce

To develop your pedagogy you need to be aware and critical of what underpinning theoretical perspectives you use to understand how children learn and develop. Many practitioners in day nurseries, child-minding settings and foundation units in school have a limited understanding of how children learn and are simply

> *technicians, who implement the educational ideas and procedures of others, rather than professionals who think of these ideas for themselves.*
>
> (Alexander, 2004, p11)

The Effective Provision of Pre-School Education (EPPE) (Sylva et al., 2004) is a long-itudinal study investigating the effects of pre-school education on three and four year olds. The report found that there was a correlation between the levels of qualifications held by the manager and a higher quality of pre-school environment. The research has suggested strong correlations between quality provision of early years education and children's later educational outcomes and between levels of professional training and the quality of early years provision. These were points reinforced by a recent report into early education and childcare qualifications (Nutbrown, 2012).

As professionals in the early years workforce we need to have a practice that is founded on sound educational values and principles and that enables us to look at curriculum policies and procedures through a critical lens. Then we can draw out from policy and curricula the best practice for young children embedded in them. This can only be achieved if we have an awareness of our own theoretical basis for our actions. Some research suggests that many practitioners working in early years settings are carrying out activities with children with limited critical understanding of the long-term value in terms of the child's learning the activity is having (Stephen, 2010).

Consider autobiographical account 4. Here I was unaware that the child was going through an important aspect of learning and using a schema to support this. With the theoretical knowledge learned through my teacher training programme I was in a position to make valuable links between theory and practice and therefore look to support the child through this schema and help to maximise the learning opportunities.

Curriculum and pedagogy

There has been in the past a confusion between the terms curriculum and pedagogy. Alexander (2004) attributes this to English educational discourse making pedagogy subsidiary to curriculum. In actual fact, he suggests, we need to consider it the other way round with *pedagogy being the act of teaching together with its attendant discourse* (Alexander, 2004, p11). The curriculum is just one of the strands of our pedagogy and as practitioners in education we certainly need a strong underlying knowledge and understanding of the curriculum requirement. However, it is the combination of our past experiences, our education and training towards education, including knowledge of curriculum requirements and our current context, that combine to develop our own personal pedagogy. This does not mean, however, that we should unthinkingly accept whatever is suggested by our curricula.

The curriculum is certainly reflected in our pedagogy but it is our underpinning knowledge of how children learn and our principles of education, what we think education is for, that enable us to effectively interpret and implement curriculum requirements. Within the early years sector play is the foundation for children's learning. However, as Wood (2010) highlights, the commitment to play in early years has always been strong on ideology and rhetoric, that is it has been more honoured in the breach than in the observance, perhaps. Some consider this to be particularly the case now, when play has to be balanced against the need to achieve standardised outcomes as measured through the Early Years Foundation Stage Profile. This can create challenges for educators in providing a *responsive and proactive curriculum* (Wood and Attfield, 2005) while having to keep one eye on the lookout for measurable outcomes that can be 'ticked off'. At times this can cause difficulties between external curriculum requirements and your beliefs and theories of how children can take control of their own learning (see Case Study 5 below).

CASE STUDY 5

Autobiographical account 5

Following my teacher training degree I went to work in a school with a head teacher whose pedagogy was reflected very strongly through a constructivist approach to learning. The creative curriculum was the vehicle that drove learning in all other curriculum areas. Construction materials were prominent through all classes from nursery to year 6. In nursery children were using Duplo and large wooden blocks, while through to year 6 the children were using technical Lego and computer-based Lego. Children's writing and maths was based on many of the creative experiences the children had encountered, enabling them to be more fully engaged in the writing process because they had lived through the process in the building section. The head teacher was very firm in her beliefs as to how children learn and develop. When new policy documents were made statutory she would look at how they could be implemented to enhance the curriculum we worked within and used them to enhance provision rather than throw out our existing ideas and start again based on the guidance. She taught me that you should stay true to your beliefs as to how children learn and the importance of having a strong underlying pedagogy that you are conscious of, being aware of your beliefs, opinions and the theoretical understandings of learning. On moving to a different school I realised how strong my personal pedagogy had become, moving from a creative curriculum where children expressed their individual ideas through their art work, to a setting that had all children painting the same picture of a flower and promoted a more formal curriculum of reading and writing with limited creativity. This caused a conflict in my personal pedagogy.

Task

How do you manage a conflict between your beliefs and opinions against external factors that have to be considered in your teaching approach?

A constructivist approach to learning

Constructivism suggests we make meaning of the world through our first-hand experience of the environment. It is based on the belief that we are actively involved in a process of learning and as learners we construct knowledge and meaning for ourselves through this process and in a strong sense 'invent the world'. This is in opposition to traditional ideas of the learner as a passive participant in the process, a 'blank slate' that is written on by the educator. Piaget was very influential in the development of the constructivist curriculum and considered that we learn through expanding our existing ideas through play and practical experiences.

What does this mean for pedagogy?

For Piaget the best form of learning was discovery learning and we can see this embedded in much early years practice today. The curriculum supports this in many ways, often promoting the use of the environment as a field for guided exploration. However, the EYFS also recognises the use of language and adult guidance in ensuring that this discovery learning does not falter as the child finds their limits of ability or their knowledge is challenged. In doing so it makes use of the ideas, or perhaps a particular interpretation of the ideas, of Vygotsky and his concept of the Zone of Proximal Development.

These ideas were covered in Chapter 3 but it is worth noting here that common to them is the idea of a pedagogy based on partnership with the child. If we are to accept children as creators, or at least co-creators, of their knowledge what does this mean for how we approach working with them? Accepting children as co-creators of knowledge means giving them some power in the process, often a difficult proposition for adults when working with children, but one that can lead to joyful and creative explorations for both adult and child and is a necessary part of any pedagogy that considers itself to be 'child-centred' (Samuelsson and Johansson, 2006).

CHAPTER SUMMARY

In this chapter we have considered the aspects of our lives that contribute and combine to develop our personal pedagogy. We have looked at factors such as our early childhood experiences and those from our own education and our understanding of education and the theoretical underpinnings of how children learn. To become aware of our own pedagogy we need to critically examine all of these as well as our own interpretation of the curriculum we need to follow and how we relate to the social context and traditions of the education systems we work within.

It is important that you develop awareness of these beliefs and approaches to teaching. Throughout your career in education you will experience new curriculum frameworks, colleagues with different approaches and beliefs to you and different learners.

Self-assessment questions
1. What are the 'invisible' influences which impact upon our pedagogical practices?
2. What are schemas? Give an example of a schema and the associated behaviours.
3. What is meant by a constructivist approach to learning?

FURTHER READING

Alexander, R (2004) Still no pedagogy? Principle, pragmatism and compliance in primary education, *Cambridge Journal of Education*, 34 (1): 7–33.

Eaude, T (2011) *Thinking Through Pedagogy for Primary and Early Years*. Exeter: Learning Matters.

Leach, J and Moon, B (eds) (1999) *Learners and Pedagogy*. London: Paul Chapman.

Leach, J and Moon, B (2008) *The Power of Pedagogy*. London: Sage.

Shulman, L (1987) Knowledge and teaching: foundations of the new reform, *Harvard Educational Review*, 57 (1): 1–22.

Stephen, C (2010) Pedagogy: the silent partner in early years learning, *Early Years*, 30 (1): 15–28.

5 Enhancing pedagogical practice
Rebecca Walters

Reading through this chapter will help you to:

- consider the specific elements in the cycle of planning, observation and assessment and how each element builds and supported other aspects;
- apply your understanding of the planning cycle to your work in the early years sector;
- identify areas for further development to be included in your action plan.

Introduction

We have seen how play is a difficult concept to define yet we have recognised through previous chapters that early childhood play is not simply about a pleasurable activity but indeed the underpinning foundations for learning to take place.

ACTIVITY 1

1. *What is play? The best way to do this may be to illustrate what distinguishes play from other activities with examples.*
2. *Consider the benefits which play offers and to what extent this is relevant through the primary years and beyond.*
3. *How does adult play differ from children's play?*

We have considered factors such as intrinsic motivation and child-led play so how do we begin to align this with the curriculum requirements? The Early Years Foundation Stage (EYFS) states that *children need to have a balance of activities led by children and led or guided by adults* (DfE, 2012b, p6). Siraj-Blatchford et al. (2002, p12) identified in her research that there are three main approaches to early education:

- the teacher-directed, programmed learning approach;
- an open framework approach where children are provided with 'free' access to a range of instructive learning environments in which adults support children's learning;
- a child-centred approach where the adults' aim is to provide a stimulating yet open-ended environment for children to play in.

Within this research they concluded that the first two approaches are the most effective in supporting children's learning. In these approaches, they discuss the importance of children having the opportunity to freely choose to play with an aspect of the learning environment, but adult intervention at points within the play is still beneficial.

Definitions

The teacher-directed, programmed learning approach

Structured play led by the adult

Practitioner delivers an activity that is planned by the adult with specific outcomes delivered to the whole class, a small group of children or an individual child. This could be the result of observations of children and an activity is planned to support the interests and developmental levels identified through observations or situated within the objectives from the planning overview linked to the topic work.

Led by children and guided by adults

An open framework approach where children are provided with 'free' access to a range of instructive learning environments in which adults support children's learning

In this type of learning approach the child has chosen to play with/in a specific activity area within the setting/classroom. The practitioner will step in and support the child through talking to them about their activity or helping them move the learning on.

Led by children/a child-centred approach

Where the adults' aim is to provide a stimulating yet open-ended environment for children to play within

The child directs their own learning, choosing the resources or areas that they want to play in. They then play in the area independently or with other children but with no adult involvement.

ACTIVITY 2

Think of each of the types of play listed above. Consider the pros and cons for each approach. Consider the impact on child development if one approach is adopted in isolation.

The dilemma for practitioners is based on making the decision as to how much intervention should the adult give and when is that intervention appropriate? Effective learning needs to consider a balance of all models of interacting in learning developed to meet the individual needs of the child.

It is perhaps, useful to look at the play types as a continuum (see Figure 5.1) with adult-led on one side and child-led on the other and a sliding movement across the two sides as to when each mode of teaching is appropriate. Within this model we need to consider a balance of the approaches. Focusing on just structured and directed play can cause us to limit children's learning and their opportunities to actively engage with their environment, while leaving the child to direct their own play with limited adult intervention can cause them to miss out on valuable learning opportunities.

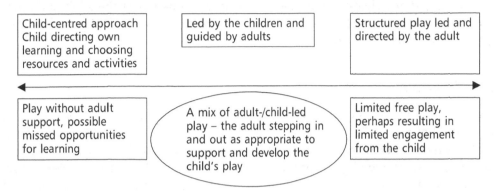

Figure 5.1 Play continuum

However, *it is very easy to misjudge – to take over a child's learning inappropriately or to miss opportunities to extend the learning through effective and timely intervention* (Allen and Whalley, 2010, p93). Consider the case study below and consider how Phoebe, a confident four year old, was able to take control of her own learning and remind the practitioner that it is easy to misjudge their behaviour.

CASE STUDY 1

Lois was a teacher in the foundation unit in a primary school. In her class she worked with children between the ages of four and five. The children had opportunities for free and unstructured play across a range of areas, such as wet and dry sand, water, large and small construction, and the home corner, to name a few. On this particular morning, Phoebe, who was four years old, was playing on her own in the home corner. She was happily dressing the dolls and making their lunch and feeding them. After a while Lois noticed that Phoebe seemed to be engaging in the same activity and it was not developing or moving on; she had stopped playing with the dolls and appeared to be 'disengaged' from the activity. Lois decided that it was time for her to refocus Phoebe's learning and re-engage her with the activity. Lois went into the home corner and started to prepare food with the pretend food resources. She put some of the food pieces in the pan and encouraged Lois to come over and make lunch for the baby because he looked hungry. At this point Phoebe walked over to Lois and took her by the hand and walked her over to the seating area in the home corner. 'You sit down there and get yourself comfortable and I will go and make you a lovely cup of tea,' said Phoebe to her teacher. Having sat Lois on the chair Phoebe promptly went back to the activity she was engaged in before the teacher interrupted her.

The balance between stepping in and supporting a child in their play and having the confidence that learning is occurring is a very difficult one to achieve. As you can see in the case study above, Phoebe was happy and content in the play she was engaged in. She saw the teacher's attempt at moving the play and learning forward as an intrusion and confidently redirected the teacher to a place that did not impact on her play. This can be achieved by providing an environment that is rich in opportunities for learning, through careful observations of children and by enabling them to engage in both adult-led and child-led activities. The danger can be that if the adult intervenes too much in order to structure the play then some of the essential features are lost, especially the child's control!

Free-flow play

All the play children engage in is structured to a point through the resources and activities that are provided in the early years environment. Moyles (1989) has argued that the term 'structured play' has not been helpful for practitioners as it creates a notion that structured play means the teacher is involved in the activity, while unstructured play has no adult involvement. It is more appropriate to consider the nature of the adult involvement. It is indeed clear that children need to engage in activities that are driven by themselves; however, there is also recognition that a balance of the two can enhance and create more challenges to learning. Bruce (2001) developed the term 'free-flow' play, when children are able to reach their *deepest and widest levels of learning*. She considered that play is about learning new skills and then being able to use these newly developed skills in a flexible and imaginative way. The adult's role in free-flow play is to plan and enable, guiding the child. She describes the conditions in which free-flow play arises through her 12 features of play (see Table 5.1). She considers that when seven or more of the features are present we are likely to see effective learning.

Table 5.1 Bruce's 12 features of free-flow play

1. Using first-hand experiences
2. Making up rules
3. Making props
4. Choosing to play
5. Rehearsing the future
6. Pretending
7. Playing alone
8. Playing together
9. Having a personal agenda
10. Being deeply involved
11. Trying out recent learning
12. Co-ordinating ideas, feelings and relationships for free-flow play

Source: Bruce (2004)

ACTIVITY 3

Choose one of the activities listed below:

- *role-play shopping;*
- *building in the large construction area;*
- *playing a board game.*

Consider if seven of the features are present. Which ones?

Do you agree that if seven features are not present in the child's play then the learning will be less effective?

Play spiral

Moyles (1989) gives us the example of the play spiral, in which the balance of child-directed and adult-led play is crucial in ensuring learning is developed. She highlights that the starting point of a play activity should always be free play, enabling the child to explore and develop confidence in the activity/resource. Following on from this when the child has had sufficient time to explore freely the play should be directed through engagement with the more knowledgeable other. In this process of directed play the child is able to upskill and develop a new understanding of the activity/resource. Through then allowing the child more free play they reconstruct and accommodate the new understanding and bring it into their play as they explore. She highlights *access to free play – that is the opportunity to explore and investigate material for oneself – can be the forerunner to more challenging play. It can and should, however, also be the sequel to it* (Moyles, 1989, p14).

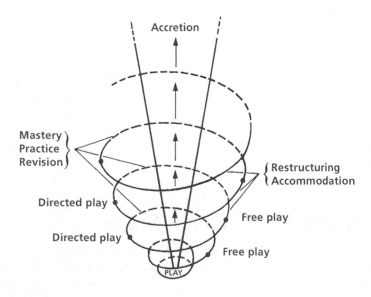

Figure 5.2 Play spiral
Source: Moyles (1989)

ACTIVITY 4

In the Tweenies room this week the theme was autumn. The practitioner took the children for an autumn walk around the local park and while out on the walk the children collected leaves and twigs. When they got back into the setting the practitioner placed the leaves and twigs in a tuff tray and allowed the children to explore them. The practitioner stepped back and allowed the children 'free play' with the materials. She observed the children for a period of time. Initially the children enjoyed feeling and touching the leaves and watching them float down. Once the children appeared comfortable and confident in exploring the materials the practitioner sat with them and added some animals to the leaves, talking about where they might live and what their habitats may look like. The teacher then stepped back and left the children to 'free play'. The children began selecting some of the woodland animals and hiding them in the leaves and making dens for them. Following some interesting discussions the children had been having together, talking about where the animals would sleep and why they were hiding, the play started to end and the children began to move to other areas to play. The following morning the teacher decided to step in and challenge the play in the leaves and move it to the next level. She read the children The Gruffalo. They talked about where the Gruffalo lives and the different creatures that the Gruffalo finds on his journey. The teacher then provided the children with the animals that are discussed in the story and she played with the children in the tuff tray retelling the story of the Gruffalo. She used the language from the book to retell the story and encouraged the children to join in and help her. After spending some time with the children she left them to play freely in the tuff tray.

Questions

How can you see the role of Vygotsky's more knowledgeable other being used in the above case study to support children's learning?

Can you identify the different stages of the play spiral?

How can the play spiral be developed further?

Through enabling the children to have opportunities to explore and play freely with the materials the children have opportunities to study them. The teacher stepping in and directing the play provides the children with a new challenge in the play that can extend their knowledge and understanding. This spiral process of free play, directed play and then enriched free play can lead to increased knowledge and mastery of practice (Moyles, 1989).

The Early Years Foundation Stage

The Early Years Foundation Stage (EYFS) is the statutory document that all practitioners in England working with children between the ages of 0 and 5 are required to work with to ensure children benefit from a safe, secure and happy environment that supports and enhances their learning and development. It is recognised that high-quality early years' experience has a lasting impact on children's life chances

(Sylva et al., 2004). The EYFS became a statutory requirement in 2008 and in 2012 was revised. The EYFS statutory framework is divided into three sections:

- learning and development;
- assessment;
- safeguarding and welfare requirements.

These three focused areas consider the statutory standards that all early years providers in England must meet to ensure children are kept safe and healthy and can learn and develop to their full potential.

The learning and development section in the EYFS is focused on supporting children's learning through play-based experiences. Seven areas of learning are outlined in this section. Three of these areas are referred to as the 'prime areas' (see Figure 5.3) and are seen as crucial *for igniting children's curiosity and enthusiasm for learning and building their capacity to learn, form relationships and thrive* (DfE, 2012b, p4). These prime areas form the underpinning foundations to support learning in all other areas. The four 'specific areas' are central to children's learning and it is through the specific areas that the prime areas are strengthened and developed and vice versa.

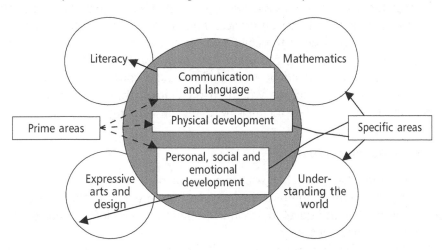

Figure 5.3 Prime areas and specific areas
Adapted from DfE (2012b)

Planning to support learning and development

Planning in the early years is about meeting young children's needs so that they can play and learn happily in ways which will help them develop skills and knowledge. The key to providing children with a challenging, varied and exciting curriculum is to work from the child's interests. The planning process forms a cycle of observation, assessment and planning. We will now look at each of these stages in turn to consider how this supports the development of a child-centred curriculum that enables the practitioner to meet the children's needs in a play-based curriculum.

Observation

Observational assessment is the way in which in our everyday practice, we observe children's learning, strive to understand it, and then put our understanding to good use.

(Drummond, 1993, p13)

Observation is the starting point for the planning cycle. *Observation is an authentic means of learning about children, what they know and what they are able to do* (Morrison, 2011, p146): it helps us as practitioners see what the child's interests are and to consider how these interests can be reflected in the planned activities we provide for children. Observations are vital as each child is unique and differs in ability. Observations can capture these differences first-hand. The starting point is always with the child, observing what the child chooses to do, what their interests are and who they choose to play with, providing valuable information about a child as an individual. Observations should be part of the regular routine and provide practitioners with opportunities to see where children are in terms of their ability and therefore plan more accurately for their next steps in learning.

Why do we observe children?

- To understand where the child is at in terms of their learning needs.
- To develop an understanding of the individual preferences and dislikes of a child.
- To be able to plan and develop activities to meet the individual needs of children in the group – differentiation.
- To identify significant changes in a child's behaviour.
- To develop our understanding of how children learn and to make the connections between theory and practice.
- To enable us as practitioners to collect information about a child in an unobtrusive way that captures the child in their natural state of learning rather than through prescribed tests and activities.
- To enable practitioners to identify effective teaching methods and to reflect on practice.
- To help us get to know our children on a more personal level so we can build relationships with them.

Observation is the starting point for collecting information about a child or a group of children, but observing children in a purposeful and meaningful way requires practitioners who are skilled and knowledgeable in the observation process. Practitioners should plan 'ongoing assessments (also known as formative assessments) as an integral part of the learning and development process. You could think of it as looking for an object in the dark – you can feel around and try to find the object; however, if you turn the light on you can go straight to it. Without observing a child we are feeling around in the dark, guessing the stage of learning they are at; however, if we have engaged in meaningful observations of the child, it is like turning on the light, and we can see the direction their learning needs to take. Put simply, observation is the practice of looking at and listening to children to find out how they are developing, it is about focusing on what the child can do, not what the child cannot do.

As well as planned observations, practitioners should also be ready to capture the spontaneous but important moments that occur as these can offer useful snapshots of a child's learning. There are several types of observation that a practitioner may engage in and they have to be able to make decisions about what is the most appropriate form to use according to the nature of the information they want to determine about a child.

Some types of observations

Running record – This is writing down everything observed about a child in a set time period. This includes rich descriptive detail such as what the child says, what he or she does and interactions with others. This type of observation is very time-consuming and it can be hard for the observer to write down all of the events but it does give a lot of detail and puts the situation in a context as everything is recorded. This therefore makes it easier for other professionals to understand the situation clearly.

Event sampling – In this type of observation the observer watches for a specified behaviour either positive or negative and then records exactly what preceded the event, what happened during the event and what the consequences of the event were. Because this type of observation is looking at cues through cause and effect it will help to address a particular behaviour!

Checklists – This is a list of predetermined behaviours or skills that the observer ticks off as they observe the child exhibiting them.

Time sample – This is a type of observation that focuses on what the child is doing at fixed periods of time. By recording a child at regular intervals over a period of time you can build up a picture of who the child is playing with, where they are choosing to play and how they move around the environment. This method of observation looks at the child at 10–15 minute intervals and gives a broad overview but can restrict the whole picture.

Tallies – These provide a record as to how often an event or a type of behaviour has occurred over a period of time.

Learning stories – A learning story is a narrative account of a series of events that link together and capture the context of the learning that is taking place. The learning story is developed over a period of time and builds a picture of the child's progress, highlighting their achievements and what will come next.

ACTIVITY 6

Consider the scenarios below and in each think about the type of observation that would be most suited to finding out about the child's learning and development:

- *How does a child move around the setting and mix with other children?*
- *Developing a portfolio of narrative about a child.*
- *A child is having some behavioural issues.*

Used in a proactive way, observations can be a dynamic approach to supporting children's learning and development.

Observations are the first stage of the planning cycle and as such, on their own, they are limited in their value. The second part of the cycle is to consider how you are going to use the observations to support and enhance the learning of the child – this is the assessment stage. This reflection on the observation is the most valuable aspect as it provides useful and useable information to inform your planning and teaching, giving you the opportunity to make judgements about what you have observed and make decisions as to how this will be reflected in the planning process.

Formative assessment is ongoing and is used to inform practitioners about the individual needs of the child and the next steps that need to be planned. Formative assessments are the ongoing observations that are collected and used to build up a picture of a child. These observations are then analysed and used to plan future learning experiences for children.

Summative assessment is a summary of the child's overall achievement produced in a formal report. In the EYFS practitioners are required to produce a summative report at two points. There is a statutory requirement for children in early years settings to have a progress check at the age of two. Within this progress check practitioners will identify the child's strengths and areas of development in the prime areas. The information from this progress check must be shared with parents in the form of a written report.

Toward the end of the Foundation Stage, in the final term of the reception class, the practitioner will provide a summative assessment of the child's development in the Early Years Foundation Stage Profile (EYFSP). This assessment sums up all the information collected through ongoing formative assessments that have been made about the child. The child's development will be assessed against the early learning goals and this information must be shared with the Year 1 teacher that the child will be progressing to and also with the parents. This information is also shared with the local authority to examine and chart against local schools.

For many these types of assessment can create a tension between an outcome-based curriculum and trying to keep a focus on the child-centred and child-led nature of practice. Some empirical work has pointed out the possible tensions in practice when a focus on 'content knowledge', that is what practitioners are told children have to be seen to have learnt, takes priority over process when that process is supposed to be based on first-hand discovery through play (Moyles et al., 2002). Play and child-centred education have often been characterised as open-ended and generating their own learning goals. To have externally generated goals placed around it can be seen by some as a useful scaffold but by others as more of a straitjacket. The revisions to the Early Years Foundation Stage are partly a response to what was seen by some as a content-heavy curriculum.

The reality is more complex than this of course, and, as Wood (2007) suggests, children themselves are striving, as they learn, to master socially and culturally appropriate tasks and ways of being. A child-centred education cannot ignore these wider social and cultural imperatives.

ACTIVITY 7

Consider the summative assessments discussed above with particular reference to those in the EYFS that measure a child's progress at the ages of two and five. How does this fit with the idea of a child-centred curriculum and a supportive play environment?

ACTIVITY 8

Consider the two types of assessment, summative and formative.

Consider the benefits of each type of assessment.

Think of a situation when summative assessment would be more appropriate and think of a situation when it would be more beneficial to use formative assessment.

When planning for the early years it is about meeting the needs of young children to help them learn and develop. Planning is the third stage of the cycle and practitioners use the observations that have been analysed and show the next stage of learning for the children. Planning is only effective when staff take into account children's needs, dispositions and stages of development. Planning takes the form of three stages: long, medium and short term.

Long-term plans look at the overview of activities and themes that will occur across a defined time scale. For some settings the long-term plan will focus on the whole year; this gives the practitioners an overview as to what they intend the children to learn. This plan will include visitors, visits out of the setting, celebrations, etc. These events provide rhythms and continuity across a defined length of time.

From the long-term plans medium-term plans are developed. These plans ensure that across a period of time, such as six weeks or a half-term, there is more detail around the specific activities you are focusing on. This stage of planning is about collecting the resources and materials needed to address the learning.

On the other hand, short-term plans are those that are informed by the ongoing assessments and observations of children and through discussions with parents, colleagues and the children. These are the daily and weekly plans that are crucial in meeting the individual needs of children. Short-term planning is about adapting the plans to meet the needs of the children and this type of planning will be subject to the current interests of the children (see Case Study 2 below).

CASE STUDY 2

The observations of children and the subsequent plans need to be flexible and used to guide and support learning rather than be adhered to rigidly. Consider the following.

Mrs Fields was a reception teacher working with children aged four and five years old. One morning she was ready with a set of activities that had been planned based around an area of the curriculum she was due to deliver. However, the children arrived at school excited about the weather – it was a cold and frosty morning with ice covering the playground and surrounding grass and garden area. Mrs Fields recognised the excitement that the first frost of the year had created with the children and how eager they were to explore it further. She decided to use this as an opportunity to enhance and engage children in their learning. When the children arrived they left their coats on and went outside to explore the frost. The looked at the frost on the pavement and on the grass and then they went into the sensory garden to look at the different patterns of frost on different sizes of shapes and leaves and plants. The children then collected some leaves to take back indoors with them. They put leaves in bowls of water which they then put in different places – one in the garden, one in the freezer, one in the shed and one in the classroom. The children then checked the bowls with the leaves at several points throughout the day to see which bowl of water turned to ice first.

ACTIVITY 9

In the case study above, what difficulties may the teacher face having abandoned her original plans?

What will the children have learned from this activity?

How could this activity be developed across other areas of learning?

The learning environment

When planning and making provision for children's learning and development we need to take into account the learning environment. This space doesn't just happen – it needs to be thought about and developed, and regardless of how much effort is spent in promoting free play there is always an element of structure that is provided through the way the resources and environment are laid out and presented. In the Reggio Emilia pre-school system, it can be seen that children learn readily from their environment which is considered to be the child's third teacher, after the parent/teacher and the child him or herself as the first two. The environment in the Reggio system is carefully planned to support a complex, varied and changing interaction between the environment and the child.

Reggio Emilia

Reggio Emilia is a small village in northern Italy in which Loris Malaguzzi (1920–94) helped to develop a pre-school education system following the Second World War. The provision was driven by a need for childcare for women to go into the workforce. At the heart of the philosophy of the Reggio approach is a powerful image of the child, who is full of potential, competent and needs to be an active participant in their learning. The teacher, parent, community and child are seen as collaborators in the learning process. Projects come from the children's interests and are driven forward as a partnership between the adult and the child.

To learn more about the Reggio approach visit Reggio Children at the following address: **www.reggiochildren.it/**.

Many theorists have considered the importance of the environment in supporting the learning and development of children through their research. Figure 5.4 presents a number of examples.

Maria Montessori
A key aspect of the Montessori approach was to have a carefully organised environment with materials and resources to enable children to develop and support their own learning. The environment is set out with resources that Montessori developed herself. The resources are clearly available in an uncluttered environment that the children can access. The Montessori environment supports the free flow of play between the indoor and outdoor environment.

Piaget
For Piaget the child's constant interactions with the environment cause them to develop and reinvent their knowledge through more complex interactions.

Rudolf Steiner
The Steiner approach places much emphasis on providing a suitable environment rich with natural and sensory resources. The resources are usually chosen to be open ended and used in a variety of ways. Emphasis is on providing a 'warm and joyful' environment (Steiner Waldorf Schools Fellowship, 2009).

Friedrich Froebel
The environment has an important role in the child's development. It must promote curiosity, stimulation and challenge. Froebel saw the outdoor environment as important for supporting children's learning as the indoor environment.

McMillan Sisters
Fresh air and exercise are at the heart of the McMillan approach to learning. The outdoor garden is essential to the overall well-being and education of the child.

Figure 5.4 Some theoretical perspectives on the importance of the environment

The environment is often the first thing that is noticed when you go into a setting: both children and adults make decisions about the setting based on their initial perceptions.

ACTIVITY 10

Imagine yourself in a child's shoes, the same height as a child looking around. You have just walked into the setting.

- *What might you see?*
- *Is there anything familiar?*
- *How easy is it to access things in the environment?*
- *How easy is it to talk to an adult and ask for help?*

These are some of the things that need to be considered when thinking about the child's needs when developing the environment as it plays a key role in supporting and developing children's learning.

For children to have rich learning experiences then the learning environment needs to be well planned and resourced. Children learn differently and the learning environment needs to reflect opportunities for the different ways that children learn. Some of the aspects that need to be considered are listed below.

- There needs to be room for children to move around freely.
- The resources and equipment need to be ordered and labelled in a way that enables children to access them independently.
- There needs to be a range of work spaces providing children with opportunities to play in groups or alone.
- There needs to be comfortable carpeted areas and quiet areas for reflection.
- Flexibility is required – be prepared to change things in order to develop and support children's learning.

The physical space should contain resources and materials that children can explore and investigate using all of their senses. It is important that some of the materials and resources should be familiar to the children from their home and community environment, while there should also be opportunities for children to engage in new materials and resources.

ACTIVITY 11

Thinking about some of the things we have discussed in terms of the physical environment, what areas would you expect to see in an early years setting?

Here are some of the areas that should be available continuously within an early years environment:

- role-play area – including a home corner as this is familiar to a child
- construction area
- mark-making/office area
- maths area
- water area
- sand area – wet and dry
- workshop area
- malleable materials
- music area
- painting area – easel, table, floor
- book corner
- IT area
- investigation.

In these areas practitioners need to consider the basic and continuous resources that are available to the children all of the time. For example, in the water tray some of the basic provision may be different sized jugs, beakers and cups as well as sieves to enable the children to explore the properties of water in a way that allows them to reinforce and develop their understanding. However, the provision could be enhanced to support the current project. For example, if the theme is floating and sinking a new set of materials may be added to enhance the work in the water to encourage the children to further develop this theme. This is enhanced provision. The important aspect of continuous and enhanced provision is that the continuous provision remains available on a daily basis, allowing the children to have free exploration with the materials. Then, through the input of the enhanced materials, the children are encouraged to challenge their learning.

ACTIVITY 12

Consider the sand tray in an early years setting.

- *What do you think the continuous provision may be?*
- *The current theme is dinosaurs. How can the materials be enhanced to support the theme and children's learning?*

The key factor for practitioners to remember is that the environment needs to be exciting and inspiring and serves to support and challenge young children across a broad and balanced curriculum. When planning for the environment practitioners needs to ask themselves 'What opportunities for learning do we want to offer the children?' As Ceppi and Zini (in Moyles, 2010, p156) highlight: *In the long term, an environment that is not stimulating, inspiring and full of energy, activity and fun will dull children's perceptions and disadvantage their learning.*

The learning environment is not just about the physical space. It also involves people, and children need to feel cared for, comfortable and relaxed. The environment is crucial to a child's learning, but it is the role of the 'educator' to facilitate this learning appropriately. As in the term 'scaffolding' used by Bruner, we need to look for and plan opportunities in children's learning to step in and extend that learning when appropriate. We can using the play spiral from Moyles to enable children to have opportunities for free play that can be enhanced through the adult stepping in at key points and challenging the learning. The adult is the pivotal factor in supporting children to feel safe and trust the adults around them. Their role is to:

- offer a range of learning experiences and resources;
- tune into the child's needs and interests;
- jointly engage in problem solving and sustained shared thinking;
- respond to observed interests;
- monitor materials, children's involvement and their own involvement with children to ensure that they offer relevant experiences;
- evaluate provision to ensure that they are providing quality learning experiences.

Sustained shared thinking

Sustained shared thinking is associated with high-quality learning experiences for children. The terminology often frightens practitioners who may not understand the language but are actually engaging in the activity in their practice. It is also useful to consider it under the terminology of a 'sustained shared conversation'. Essentially it is a conversation between adults and children in which they both have a genuine interest and desire to work together to find out more about something, solve a problem or an activity. Siraj-Blatchford et al. define it as *an episode when two or more individuals (children together, or adults and children) work together in an intellectual way to solve a problem, clarify a concept, evaluate activities or extend a narrative, etc. Both parties must contribute to the thinking, and it must develop and extend* (2002, p8).

Below is an example of sustained shared thinking:

(Maisie and Jessica (the teacher) are working in the sticking area together.)

Maisie: I think I would like to build a car.

Jessica: That's a good idea. What do you think we should use to build the car?

Maisie: A box?

Jessica: Yes. We could use the box for the main shape of the car. I am not sure what we could use for the wheels though. *(Jessica and Maisie have a look through some of the containers containing the scrap modelling materials.)*

Maisie: I know, look some bottle tops, they could be the wheels.

Jessica: Why would they be good for the wheels?

Maisie: Because they are round.

Jessica: Yes, good idea, wheels on a car are round so that they can turn round. We could stick them on the side of the box for the wheels.

Maisie: Yes. We need to find four.

Jessica: Yes, four that are the same size.

(*Maisie looks through and finds four green bottle tops all the same size.*)

Maisie: Do you think this glue will stick them to the side of the box?

Jessica: Let's have a go. (*They each put some glue onto one of the bottle tops and attach it to the side of the box.*) Oh no, it is sliding off!

Maisie: Shall I hold it for a little bit to see if it will stick?

Jessica: That's a good idea.

In the dialogue above, Jessica and Maisie are working in a collaborative way to solve a problem together. They have a starting point and through the discussion and dialogue have developed and extended the learning to build the model car.

When we discuss the early years environment we are considering both the indoor and the outdoor environment. The indoor and outdoor environment should be seen as connected by the children and adults inhabiting the space (Williams-Siegfredson, 2012, p44) and should both be available, when the environment allows it, enabling the children to move freely between the two. This is where the term 'outdoor classroom' was introduced to emphasise the importance of the outdoor environment, but for some this created an understanding that the indoor classroom should be duplicated outside. However, we need to consider the outdoor space as an area that offers something extra to the indoor environment. Inside children may enjoy painting on an easel; however, we don't just want to pull the easel outside. The outside offers opportunities to make the painting bigger and on a larger scale. Don't fall into the trap of simply recreating the indoor space outside – look for opportunities to extend the learning in this space and utilise the unique opportunities for learning the outdoor environment offers.

Parental partnership

Throughout this chapter we have considered aspects of enhancing learning for children through high-quality play experiences, planning, assessment and observation and the importance of a high-quality learning environment. However, when it comes to understanding a child and knowing the unique qualities and abilities that a child has, perhaps the most important and key person to provide this information is the parent. Parents are *children's first and most enduring educators* (DCSF, 2008a), it is recognised that working together with parents can provide practitioners with a good understanding of the child's needs and have a positive impact on children's development. Research highlights that parental involvement in their child's learning positively affects the academic performance of children (Fan and Chen, 2001).

Therefore as practitioners working in the early years we need to ensure that we are working closely with parents to achieve the best possible outcomes for children.

ACTIVITY 13

We need to ensure we are sensitive to the needs of parents. Remember that when a parent entrusts their child to your care they are leaving the most precious thing in their life with you.

- *How do you ensure that the parent feels safe and secure in the knowledge that you will give their child the highest levels of care and education?*

- *How do you ensure that the parent has the opportunity to see what activities their child has been involved in while in your care?*

- *How do you ensure that parents are given the opportunity to share their thoughts and ideas with you about their child's development?*

Parents know more about their child than you do, therefore observations, planning and assessment of children should be shared with parents, enabling them to have the opportunity to add their opinions and understanding of their children to the process. Parents may be able to shed light on aspects and situations in their child's life that you have limited understanding of. For example, a bereavement in the family may cause a child's behaviour to suddenly change; however, if you have had a dialogue with a parent about this you can work to support the child through this difficult time.

Learning journals or home/setting diaries which include photographs are one of the ways to share information with a parent. This enables the parent to see some of the activities that their child has been engaged in while also being able to respond and add useful information from the child's home experiences.

ACTIVITY 14

Can you think of any other ways that a setting can work with parents to develop a partnership to support the learning and development of their child?

CHAPTER SUMMARY

In this chapter we have considered how children's learning is enhanced through play by considering the nature of play and the different aspects of play. We have considered how practitioners can plan and support children's learning through high-quality observations, assessments and planning procedures. In order to develop and enhance children's early learning experiences it is important that you develop your understanding of these aspects of early years practice.

CHAPTER SUMMARY *continued*

In thinking about the competing agendas between a play-based curriculum and an outcome-driven curriculum, a final word from Peters (1965, p110) may encourage you to consider the real underlying philosophy of education:

To be educated is not to have arrived at a destination; it is to travel with a different view. What is required is not feverish preparation for something that lies ahead, but to work with a precision, a passion and a taste at worthwhile things that lie at hand.

Self-assessment questions

1. Consider the different types of observation we have looked at in this chapter. How can they be used and adapted for different situations when working and supporting children's learning and development?
2. Think about the importance of play in the early years curriculum. What are some of the difficulties in implementing a play-based curriculum in relation to an outcome-driven curriculum?

FURTHER READING

Allen, S and Whalley, M (2010) *Supporting Pedagogy and Practice in Early Years Settings*. Exeter: Learning Matters.

Andrews, M (2013) *Exploring Play for Early Childhood Studies*. Exeter: Learning Matters.

Broadhead, P, Howard, J and Wood, E (eds) (2010) *Play and Learning in the Early Years: From Research to Practice*. London: Sage.

Drummond, MJ (1993) *Assessing Young Children's Learning*. London: David Fulton.

Moyles, JR (2010) *The Excellence of Play*, 3rd edn. Maidenhead: Open University Press.

Samuelsson, IP and Johansson, E (2006) Play and learning – inseparable dimensions in pre-school practice, *Early Child Development and Care*, 176 (1): 47–65.

Siraj-Blatchford, I, Sylva, K, Muttock, S, Gilden, R and Bell, D (2002) *Researching Effective Pedagogy in the Early Years*, Research Report RR356. DCFS. Available at: **www.dfes.gov.uk/research/data/uploadfiles/RR356.pdf**

Tickell, C (2012) *The Early Years: Foundations for Life, Health and Learning. An Independent Report on the Early Years Foundation Stage to Her Majesty's Government*. London: DfE.

6 Becoming a reflective practitioner
Rebecca Walters

Reading through this chapter will help you to:

- critically reflect upon your understanding of the terms reflection and reflective practice;
- critically explore the reflective process and apply it to your early years practice;
- identify areas for further development to be included in your action plan.

Introduction: defining reflection

We reflect on a daily basis, and much of this is through the process of quiet and thoughtful pauses or internal conversations. We look back and consider:

- What went well?
- What didn't go well?
- Why?
- How do I feel about this?

We do not usually have a set formula or structured approach, it just happens. Sometimes we might choose to do something different based on our loose processing of thoughts and feelings about an event or experience, or we might choose not to. This kind of reflective thinking and learning may range from the relatively banal – for example, you may have decided that tomorrow you are going to try a different route to work as the traffic on your normal route has been exceptionally busy – to the more personal – such as thinking about how to approach tackling a difficult subject with a friend or relative who has a tendency to be sensitive about such things.

ACTIVITY 1

Consider some of the events that have happened during this last week. Was there any time when you sat back and thought about events and considered how you would do them differently in a future context? Or was there anything that played on your mind, causing you to think about it a lot?

In the course of our day we can have many tricky events and situations that we have to deal with, but reflection is not simply looking back at the day's events in a passive fashion. It involves running back through the actions/conversations/feelings involved in a manner that can be defined as active, in the sense of seeking to evaluate or give rise to change, and systematic, in the sense of following a pre-planned pattern. Reflection is a dynamic process that involves an active engagement with knowledge and experience, because, as Gibbs says, *it is not sufficient simply to have an experience in order to learn; without reflecting upon this experience it may be quickly forgotten or its learning potential lost* (1988, p9). It is reflection on the experience and then using a new understanding of the situation to improve and develop our future actions.

Reflection is a term that has become increasingly popular in the world of education. Practitioners are encouraged to reflect as part of their professional development and as a way of developing and enhancing their practice. It is seen by many practitioners in the field of education as being at the very heart of the development of professional competence and this chapter will explain why as well as how it can become a central part of your practice. This necessitates a different approach to reflection to the day-to-day reflection that we engage in.

ACTIVITY 2

Before we begin to explore the notion of reflection and how it supports practice, first consider what we mean by the term – and the benefits for practitioners and learners.

There is no universal definition of reflection. However, there are broad acceptances of what it means. Moon (2001) uses an extract from *Harry Potter and the Goblet of Fire* as an excellent example to define reflection:

> *Harry stared at the stone basin. The contents had returned to their original, silvery white state, swirling and rippling beneath his gaze.*
>
> *'What is it?' Harry asked shakily.*
>
> *'This? It is called a Pensieve,' said Dumbledore. I sometimes find, and I am sure you know the feeling, that I simply have too many thoughts and memories crammed into my mind.'*
>
> *'Err,' said Harry who couldn't truthfully say that he had ever felt anything of the sort.*
>
> *'At these times,' said Dumbledore, indicating the stone basin, 'I use the Pensieve. One simply siphons the excess thoughts from one's mind, pours them into a basin, and examines them at one's leisure. It becomes easier to spot patterns and links, you understand, when they are in this form.'*
>
> (Rowling, 2000)

It would be a useful trick for to be able to lift out our thoughts and memories and spend some time simply looking at them, examining them from the perspective of an outsider, considering how to understand our and others' past selves and develop our future actions. Unfortunately the Pensieve only exists in the fictional world of Hogwarts and Harry Potter but the principles of reflection embedded within this passage can be the basis for reflective practice. Boud et al. (1985, p43) define reflection as *an important human activity in which people recapture their experience, think about it, mull over and evaluate it. It is this working with experience that is important in learning.*

The defining factor of reflective practice, making it different to simply looking back and reflecting on the day, is that you think about and critically analyse actions and events, with the goal of changing and improving practice through a *deliberate and purposeful act of thinking* (Loughran, 1996, p14). Boud et al. (1985) developed a model to understand the process of reflection focusing on three stages (see Figure 6.1):

- returning to the experience;
- attending to the feelings;
- re-evaluating the experience in the light of the stages and the learner's intent and self-knowledge, bringing in new knowledge that has been gained through the process.

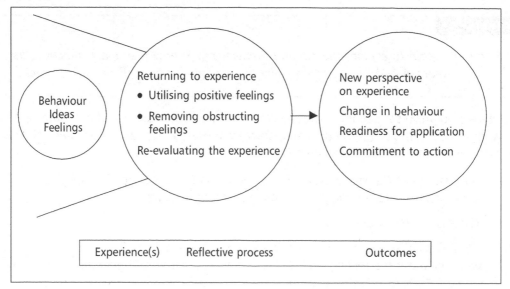

Figure 6.1 Reflective practice

Source: Boud et al. (1985)

CASE STUDY 1

Millie was a teacher in the foundation unit in a primary school. In her class she worked with children between the ages of four and five. The children had opportunities for free and unstructured play across a range of areas, such as wet and dry sand, water, large and small construction and the home corner, to name but a few. On this particular morning, Neve, who was four years old, was playing on her own in the home corner. She was happily dressing the dolls and making their lunch and feeding them. After a while Millie noticed that Neve seemed to be engaging in the same activity and it was not developing or moving on; she had stopped playing with the dolls and appeared to be 'disengaged' from the activity. Millie decided that it was time for her to refocus Neve's learning and re-engage her with the activity. Millie went into the home corner and started to prepare food with the pretend food resources. She put some of the food pieces in the pan and encouraged Neve to come over and make lunch for the baby because he looked hungry. At this point Neve walked over to Millie and took her by the hand and walked her over to the seating area in the home corner. 'You sit down there and get yourself comfortable and I will go and make you a lovely cup of tea,' said Neve to her teacher. Having sat Millie on the chair Neve promptly went back to the activity she was engaged in before the teacher interrupted her.

ACTIVITY 3

Looking at the case study above about Millie, how could she use reflective practice to develop her practice?

Was she right to step in and try to move the learning along? What might she do differently next time and why? Think about the stages that Boud et al. suggest and use this to frame the process.

Key thinkers around reflection

There have been two key thinkers associated with the development of reflective practice, John Dewey (1859–1952) and Donald Schön (1930–97). Their writings have contributed significantly to the development of reflective practice in education.

Dewey reminds us that *reflection is a complex, rigorous, intellectual and emotional enterprise that takes time to do well* (Rodgers, 2002, p844). In his book *How We Think* (1910) Dewey outlines some of his ideas on reflection and reflective practice. He identified reflection as a specialised form of thinking that sits in contrast with 'routine action'. Routine action is the normal day-to-day routines that are followed; they rest on habit, tradition and imitation and are compliant with the expectations of the professional in the workplace. Routine action is, by definition, very static and limited in its ability to change and develop.

Dewey considers the notion of 'reflective action' in contrast to this. Reflective action involves a willingness to engage in *active, persistent and careful consideration of any belief or supposed form of knowledge in the light of the grounds which support it and the further conclusions to which it tends* (Dewey, 1910, p6). This means that this type of reflective thinking starts from a position of doubt, perplexity or hesitation in or about a situation, which causes you to step back and engage in purposeful thought and enquiry in order to resolve these feelings. Engaging in this reflective way of thinking separates you from the normal 'routine action' and so both avoids repeating the situation and raises the possibility of learning from it. Dewey talks about *thinking the problem out* in order to develop ideas and a hypothesis to test out and develop the situation. The process involves:

- describing the experience;
- articulating questions from the experience;
- formulating a hypothesis;
- taking rationalised, intelligent actions to test the hypothesis through modifying the practice;
- measuring whether the practice improved by reflecting on the results.

To enable us to become effective in our teaching we need to consider the application of reflection to our everyday practices. It is through this application of reflection that we learn about and, therefore, improve and develop our practices.

Donald Schön was a key figure in this field following the work he carried out individually and with Chris Argyris around the area of reflective practice. He considered there to be different levels of reflection. He described the process of reflection in practice as a process of observing and thinking about our actions and making adjustments *as* we think about them. He said that professionals constantly face challenges in their everyday work and need to make appropriate adjustments. To do this means building reflection into action, as part of *the spontaneous, intuitive performance of actions of everyday life* (Schön, 1983, p49) and of *thinking on your feet* (Schön, 1983, p54). However, he also stressed that professionals need to have a deeper form of reflection that moves beyond our experience. This he considered to be a deeper form of reflection: reflection-on-action. This type of reflection takes place after the event, when we sit back and look at experience in more detail, considering the strengths of the action and the possible areas of development. This form of deeper reflection results in 'retrospective sense-making', which enables you then to plan changes to practice.

Professional practice is, of course, quite 'messy' in real life. It rarely follows set patterns and routines and when it does we all know as educators that, far from this being the sign of a 'well-oiled machine', it can be the sign of a lack of innovation and creativity leading to stagnation and boredom. Managing to be creative and spontaneous but also to reach goals and work together with others depends, Schön says, on engaging in the 'professional artistry' of reflective practice. For Schön, reflection-in-action is the core of professional artistry that hinges on the range and variety that the practitioner brings to unfamiliar situations, using intuition and on-the-spot thinking to help manage situations. You may not be surprised to learn that in his spare time Schön was an accomplished jazz musician, where the music-making depends upon individual improvisation within a communally agreed form.

CASE STUDY 2

Schön talks about reflection-in-action as *thinking on your feet* (Schön, 1983, p54). This ability to stop and think in the midst of action, enabling the action to be changed or enhanced in order to develop and improve the teaching opportunities. Within this model practitioners demonstrate the use of intuitive and artistic approaches in uncertain situations. Consider the case study below.

Ruth was an early years professional working in the pre-school room of a private day nursery. The previous day Ruth had been observing one of her key children, Hattie, and had highlighted how this child had shown a lot of interest in dolphins as she has just seen some on a recent holiday she had been on. Based on the information collected from this observation Ruth decided to set up an activity in the water tray with a selection of dolphins and other sea creatures. The activity was set up before the day started; however, when the children arrived at the nursery, Max, another of Ruth's key children, was extremely excited about a feather he had found on his walk there. Max was showing the other children his feather and they were talking about where it had come from. The group of children, including Hattie, were fascinated to watch the feather drift to the ground. Ruth had prepared activities for the morning following up on the interests Hattie had shown from the previous day, but this morning she was completely engrossed in the investigation of Max's feather. Ruth had a moment's pause to decide what to do. She could either continue with the planned sea creatures activity or work with the children to capture and capitalise on the excitement of the feather. Ruth decided to leave the sea creature activity for another time and follow the children's excitement at the feather. They spent the morning looking at how slowly the feather floated to the floor and compared this to other objects dropped from the same height. The children then wanted to find out the type of bird the feather had come from and they set about trying to find this in books, learning about different types of birds and where they came from.

Task
Can you identify from the case study above examples of reflection-in-action and reflection-on-action?

Deep and surface learning in relation to reflective practice

Marton et al. (1997) discuss the idea of deep and surface learning (see Figure 6.2). Surface learning is when we engage in learning by rote, for example, or see knowledge as compartmentalised and take into account as little of its context as possible, enough, say, to get us through an exam or an essay with limited engagement with or attempt to understand in depth the underlying concepts. We may learn the basic facts to get us through a situation, for example to follow a set of instructions or pass a test, but this does not provide a thorough and lasting knowledge or understanding of the context this knowledge is situated within, meaning we may not be able to repeat the demonstration of learning or transfer it to other situations. Surface learning is linked with memorising facts and a superficial retention of ideas. However, these facts are often quickly forgotten and can coincide with a failure to thoroughly understand the under-lying concepts and how to apply them. In contrast to this, a deep approach to learning involves the critical analysis of new concepts by linking them to prior knowledge and principles, making connections to other related areas of knowledge and using this new knowledge to aid in problem-solving and the construction of new ways of orienting oneself to the external environment. This type of learning promotes a more thorough understanding of the concepts being considered and a long-term retention of the concepts that enables them to be used for further problem-solving in unfamiliar con-texts. Reflective practice is part of and aids this deep learning because it involves thinking about an experience at a deeper level and in an ordered fashion.

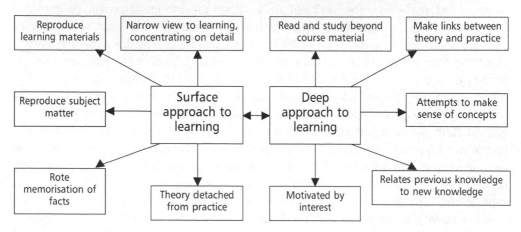

Figure 6.2 Deep and surface learning

Reflective models

A number of models of reflection have been developed to help practitioners work through the reflective process in a systematic fashion. Kolb (1984) is well known for the development of the his Experiential Learning Cycle (see Figure 6.3).

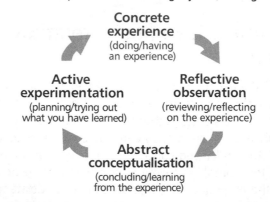

Figure 6.3 Kolb's experiential learning cycle
Adapted from Marton et al. (1997)

Source: Clara Davies **www.ldu.leeds.ac.uk/ldu/sddu_multimedia/kolb/static_version.php**

In this model we usually start with the person carrying out a particular action or having an experience and looking back through this experience at what happened. Reflecting on the events that formed the experience is the second step and needs to focus on understanding the relationship between the different component parts of the experience: who did/said what, in what order and, at the simplest level, how each of these actions lead to or structure the ensuing ones. This allows the reflector to consider how, if one of these actions had been different, the pattern of activity after could have taken a different path. From this we can begin to make plans to change and develop future actions and so finally implement the changes and see if they work. Upon reaching this point we then move back to the beginning of the reflective cycle to start the process again. Kolb argues that the cycle can start at any point but it needs to be completed for the reflective process to be meaningful.

Gibbs' (1988) reflective cycle is often used in the field of education and nursing (see Figure 6.4). It is based on Kolb's experiential cycle but incorporates the emotional content of the experience and looks at how this influences the reflective process. Within this cycle, theory and practice enrich each other by making the practitioner consider the events in the description and feelings/thoughts but then in the analysis stage to consider how the theoretical perspectives support the practice.

Figure 6.4 Gibbs' cycle breakdown
Source: Gibbs (1988)

Stage 1: Description of the event – Describe in detail the event you are reflecting on. You may consider questions such as: where were you? what were you doing? who else was involved and what were they doing? what did you say to each other and why . . .?

Stage 2: Feelings – This stage is to focus on what you were feeling at the time of the event, trying to recall what was going on inside your head. You may want to include questions such as: how are you feeling about the event now? what were you thinking at the time of the event and how did it make you feel? what were you thinking at the start and the end of the event? are you aware of how others may have been feeling and how was this communicated to you?

Stage 3: Evaluation – In this stage of the cycle you are to evaluate or make a judgement about what has happened. Consider what was good about the experience and what didn't go so well and how could things have been improved.

Stage 4: Analysis – Break the event down into its component parts so that they can be explored separately. In this section you may need to ask more detailed questions about the answers you developed in the last section. You will be focusing on what went well and what you did well

Stage 5: Conclusion – This differs from the evaluation stage in that you have explored the issue and looked at it from different perspectives to enable you to make conclusions about your own personal situation and practice. The purpose of reflection is to learn from the experience. This stage in the cycle is important as, without going through a detailed analysis and honest exploration of all the previous stages it is unlikely that you will have considered all aspects of the event, and this is the point at which we begin to learn from experience. During this stage you need to ask yourself what you could have done differently and what might have happened if you had.

Stage 6: Action plan – This stage enables you to consider, if you encountered this type of event or situation again, how would you plan to do it differently or, with all aspects of the cycle considered in depth, would you do it in a similar fashion again?

The Gibbs' cycle encourages you to think systematically about an event or situation. It is important that you progress through all of the stages of the cycle to engage in a deep and honest reflective process. Through the process of engaging with the stages in the Gibbs' reflective cycle you move beyond simply describing events and situations to engaging at a deeper level on the effect the experience has had on you, the learning that has occurred and your future learning needs.

CASE STUDY 3

The diagram below demonstrates how Millie, the Foundation teacher from Case Study 1 earlier in this chapter, could use the Gibbs' reflective cycle to consider the events that occurred and how the different stages in the cycle guide Millie into reflecting on the situation, causing her to think about aspects of theory, such as her knowledge and understanding of observation and its purpose, and how she can better use this to support her in future pedagogical contexts. Through using the cycle it also serves to highlight to Millie the successful aspects of how she engaged in the situation, allowing, for example, the child to take control of the learning situation. Displaying an openness to creativity and child-centred learning many would see as crucial to a play-based curriculum (Samuellsson and Johansson, 2006).

Description
Millie was watching Neve playing in the home corner. Millie noticed that Neve's play seemed to be repetitive – she was sat dressing and undressing the baby – so Millie felt there was an opportunity to develop the play further. Millie went into the home corner and encouraged Neve to use the kitchen area and play food to make a meal for the baby. Neve took Millie's hand and moved her to the seating area and went back to dressing and undressing the baby.

Feelings

Millie wanted to ensure that Neve was gaining as much from the learning experience as possible. She felt that by stepping into the play with Neve she could help her to access other aspects of play in this area. Millie was very surprised at how Neve had taken control of her intervention and removed her from the play. This caused Millie to wonder whether she should continue to try and encourage Neve to play with the food or to let Neve lead her own learning.

Evaluation

This incident caused Millie to consider her approach towards child-led play and the role of adult intervention. She felt sure that, as the adult, she understood the appropriate times to step in and intervene with a child's learning. However, it caused her to realise that it is a very fine balance knowing when it is appropriate to step in and move a child's learning along and when that stepping in becomes interference.

Analysis

Janet Moyles (1989) introduced us to the concept of the play spiral (see Chapter 4 for further details on this). According to Moyles the starting point should always be free play, enabling the child to explore and develop confidence in the activity/resource. The child should be given sufficient time to explore the activity/resource before the adult steps in to direct the play and move it on, thereby developing a new understanding of how the activity/resource can be used. Looking at Millie's role in stepping in and trying to develop the new focus for the play she underestimated the time element Neve required and did not give her sufficient time to explore the dolls herself. Once Neve removed Millie from her activity and Millie realised that Neve was not ready to be moved on, Millie stepped back and allowed Neve some more time in her own free play.

Conclusion

Looking back on this incident Millie can now see that she moved into support Neve in her play too soon. She should have ensured she had observed her sufficiently to see that although she appeared to be repeating the activity, in terms of Vygotsky's Zone of Proximal Development (see p43) she was possibly refining and developing her skills and was still focused on this. It helped Millie to recognise that it is important to give the child time to develop their learning.

Action plan

In future Millie will try to spend more time observing the situation to gain greater insight into the learning situation to enable her make more informed choices in supporting children's free play and adult-directed play.

The end . . . or is it?

This may be the conclusion of a single learning experience for Millie. However, this is also the beginning of her development . . . the action plan signals the beginning of another reflective cycle – what will happen next time when she is in a similar situation. The Gibbs' cycle can then be used again to support the ongoing learning and development.

Jasper talks about the need for a constant, cyclical process for reflection to develop and move on, noting that *we rarely stop at just one cycle of reflection* (Jasper, 2003, p3).

When completing the first cycle we then take action based on our reflection and, therefore, when we repeat it or a similar experience, then we do so in a new and different way (Jasper, 2003). Jasper combines reflective cycles and represents them in a continuous cycle (see Figure 6.5).

Reflective spiral

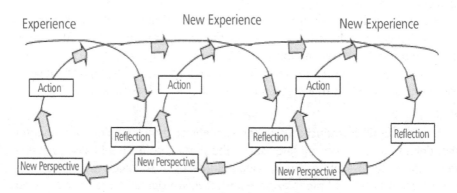

Figure 6.5 Jasper's continuous cycles of reflection
Source: Jasper (2003)

Why reflect and what do we reflect on?

Reflective practice is about formulating our loose types of mental processing into a more structured approach that pushes the practitioner to look in depth at an incident and find ways to develop, learn and improve their practice in the future. Reflective practice is a means of learning and an important strategy for professionals to promote their own professional and personal development.

We may recognise that reflective practice is engaging in thoughtful and structured activity to improve our actions in an event or situation, but how should we choose which types of event and situation to reflect on?

ACTIVITY 4

Consider the events and activities that you have engaged in during this week. Think of an event that particularly stands out for you: this can be a positive or a negative event. Use Gibb's model above and work through the different stages of the cycle using your chosen experience. Use the key questions in each of the stages to guide you through the cycle.

ACTIVITY 4 *continued*

Has the cycle helped you to develop and improve your ideas of how to manage such an experience in the future or, perhaps, transfer its positive aspects to other situations or environments?

Now do the same using Kolb's experiential learning cycle.

- *Does it look different?*
- *Which model do you prefer?*

The bigger picture in reflection

Any experience can be used as the focus for reflection; however, in professional practice we choose events that have some significance for us, in the same way that, in the above exercise, you chose an event that was significant for you during your past week. We refer to these events and experiences as 'critical incidents', significant occurrences within teaching and learning that you consider important. Brookfield (1995) describes critical incidents as situations or events that are vividly remembered and hold special significance for the writer. This structured and deliberate review of significant events has been advocated as a useful way to encourage reflection (Brookfield, 1995). The term 'critical incident' suggests something dramatic but this is not necessarily the case. A 'critical incident' is one that has significance for you, an event that made you stop and think, raised questions for you to deliberate over, or caused you to question an aspect of your beliefs, values or attitudes.

Throughout this chapter we have considered the language of reflection and how we can begin to use structured models to support us in the reflective process. However, there is a limit as to what each of us can do on our own. Brookfield (1995) widened the reflective process by considering reflection through four different lenses, causing us to consider events through a social approach to reflection, as well as through an autobiographical one. He suggests that we employ four critical lenses to view and reflect upon our practice.

- our own view (autobiographical lens) – focusing on our own experiences as a practitioner and a learner and the assumptions that shape our practice (pedagogy);
- that of our students/learners – engaging with student views;
- that of our fellow professionals;
- the various theoretical perspectives within educational literature.

He suggests that the autobiographical lens or self-reflection is the foundation of the reflective process. However, this needs to be looked at from as many different vantage points as possible and we should be engaging in each of the four lenses, causing the process to go much deeper than questioning what worked well and pushing us to consider other perspectives. He maintained the importance of dialogue among colleagues as part of the reflective process. Critical friends can be used to help shape and frame our reflection processes. Critical friendship can be defined as:

> *A trusted person who asks provocative questions, provides data to be examined through another lens, and offers critiques of a person's work as a friend. A critical friend takes the time to fully understand the context of the work presented and the outcomes that the person or group is working toward.*

(Costa and Kallick,1993, p50)

The critical friend is different to the relationship you have with a personal friend. The critical friend is there to support and guide you in an honest and trusting way, in order to develop and enhance the learning and teaching practices you engage in. This is provided through a mix of support and challenge. This person is similar but not the same as a mentor and *prompts the other person towards honest reflection and reappraisal. This may be challenging and uncomfortable, yet enhancing* (Swaffield, 2007, p1). The relationship is not one of being overfamiliar or collusive, but one in which you can work together towards a constructive critique of your professional practice.

John's model for structured reflection (2009) supports the use of a critical friend or 'supervisor' for students to be guided by and work with throughout the learning experience. He refers to this as guided reflection, *a co-developmental and collaborative research process* (2002). He considers that through sharing reflections on learning and teaching experiences, greater understanding of these can be experienced than reflecting on them alone. He has developed a framework that uses five cue questions which are then broken down into more specific /focused questions to promote a more detailed reflection.

If reflective practice is to be done properly, though, perhaps it needs to be social and part of a whole setting's practice, something that clearly depends upon a management ethos that promotes openness and honesty but also welcomes 'mistakes' as part of the process of learning to be an educator.

Thinking about social interaction

What happens when we interact with other people and how complex or simple is the process? The philosopher George Herbert Mead and, later, the sociologist Herbert Blumer suggested a way of understanding the process that has been called 'symbolic interactionism'. This suggests that when we act or speak we do so by first interpreting the action or predisposition of the other person/people we are acting towards and that these actions and utterances are conscious – that is 'rehearsed' or intended to produce a particular response. However, this action and speech has to adapt to every new action or utterance by the other and start again in each new social interaction – hence, for example, the importance of greetings in social intercourse. So talking to other people involves everyone taking part interpreting, planning and acting as part of an ongoing process.

This interaction is made more complex by the fact that we have conscious selves that we act towards. We can be angry with ourselves, blame ourselves or be pleased with our actions, for example. We can take the role of the other, taking their view into account, and we can also act towards others on the basis of what we think is or might be their view of us, deciding on our actions by thinking about the effect of them or their view of us in other words.

This makes the whole process quite complex and suggests extra layers of interaction to those that might appear to be there on the surface. It also suggests that in any social situation the meaning of it is one that is negotiated between the people involved and that in every situation we are consciously and creatively playing a role or roles.

How might this help you reflect?

- Think about the social role(s) you were playing in a particular interaction. Were you acting just as professional colleague? If so what type of colleague? One that needs help/gives advice/constructively criticises?
- What role did the other person appear to be in?
- Did either of these roles change? Did you also play the part of friend or confidant at any point?
- What prompted the change of roles and what was the effect of it on the interaction?
- What change or reinforcement of roles in the ongoing relationship between you and others was the result of a particular interaction?

Problems with reflective practice

Throughout this chapter we have considered some of the potential benefits to practice through engaging in the process of reflective practice. However, there are some barriers and problems that can prevent or make it difficult to engage in the reflective process.

Time can become one of the biggest issues for professionals engaging in reflective practice. To develop reflection at a deeper and more thorough level of thought processes that can ultimately lead to learning needs time and structure. In the life of the busy early years practitioner time is at a premium and it can make the process of reflection more difficult to engage in. Reflection can be taxing and difficult and without the necessary time and effort it can become a bland process that is based on routine and limited thinking rather than a powerful tool that can empower and transform practice.

Reflective practice is about being honest and able to look closely and openly at practice. Practitioners often forget that in looking at practice it is important to consider the strengths as well as the weaknesses. If a practitioner is constantly looking at the weaknesses in practice and not focusing on the strengths it can lead to self-doubt about practice which may cause levels of vulnerability and unrealistic expectations about the process of reflection. This can ultimately mean that the reflective process may lack impact in terms of developing and improving practice. If it is to be done properly, though, perhaps it needs to be social and part of a whole setting's practice, something that clearly depends upon a management ethos that promotes openness and honesty but also welcomes 'mistakes' as part of the process of learning to be an educator.

CHAPTER SUMMARY

In this chapter we have considered reflection along with structured models for guiding reflective practice. In order to develop and enhance your practice when working with young children you need to look at your practice and focus on both the strengths and weaknesses.

Self-assessment questions

1. How would you begin to consider reflective practice as a useful tool in supporting your practice within the early years sector for:
   (a) the practitioner?
   (b) the children?
2. What do you consider some of the difficulties in implementing reflective practice in your work with young children?

The following chapters will be considering practice in early years settings. As you work through the chapters consider how elements of reflective practice can be used to support and develop the issues and concepts being considered. Whatever our age or stage of development we are never at the end of the learning process. Engaging in reflective practice can help to remind us that there is no end point to learning (Driscoll and Teh, 2001, p98).

FURTHER READING

Jasper, M (2003) *Becoming a Reflective Practitioner: Foundations in Nursing and Health*. Cheltenham: Nelson Thornes.

Johns, C (2004) *Becoming a Reflective Practitioner*, 2nd edn. Oxford: Blackwell.

Loughran, JJ (1996) *Developing Reflective Practice: Learning About Teaching and Learning Through Modeling*. Washington, DC: Falmer.

Moon, J (2004) *A Handbook of Reflective and Experiential Learning: Theory and Practice*. Abingdon: RoutledgeFalmer.

Paige-Smith, A and Craft, A (2011) *Developing Reflective Practice in the Early Years*, 2nd edn. Maidenhead: McGraw-Hill.

7 Creating inclusive environments

Rose Envy

Reading through this chapter will help you to:

- critically reflect upon your own skills and the influence these have upon inclusive practice;

- critically appraise the notion of inclusive practice, relating this to good practice in the early years;

- apply your understanding of inclusive practice to early years practice and identify areas for development to be included in your personal development action plan.

Introduction: defining inclusion

Before we begin to look at the legislative frameworks which influence inclusive early years practice let us first explore our own understanding of inclusion.

ACTIVITY 1

What do we mean by inclusion? Write down your own definition of inclusion.

Generally, the term inclusion is used more often than not in reference to children who have special educational needs (SEN) or disabilities. However, inclusion is not just about ensuring that children with SEN and disabilities are able to participate in play and learning activities and achieve their full potential, it is about ensuring that *all* children have their individual needs met whatever their circumstance so that they can achieve their full potential. The United Nations Educational, Scientific and Cultural Organisation (UNESCO, 1994) supports and welcomes diversity among all learners. Earlier in Chapter 1 we acknowledged that *children in England are more ethnically diverse than any other age group* (Dunnell, 2007, p5), which reinforces the importance of supporting and ensuring that all children are given the opportunity to fully participate in activities which meet their individual needs, and includes children from BME groups, including those from Gypsy, Roma and Traveller families (GRTF). DfE (2010) stated that children from GRTF were the lowest achieving ethnic group within schools in England and are more likely to have SEN.

ACTIVITY 2

Why do you think that GRTF are the lowest achieving ethnic group?

Given the transient nature (frequently moving from one place to another, staying in one place for short periods of time) of GRTF, there is a lack of continuity in children's education as they can attend more than one school in any one academic year. This results in a lack of continuity in their education, children experiencing difficulties in establishing relationships with practitioners and also in establishing meaningful friendships with other children outside the GRT community. DfES (2003) states of those GRTF who did not live in permanent housing approximately one-fifth had no secure place to live. Under normal circumstances some children experience difficulties when they transition, that is move from one educational phase to another, for example from nursery to reception or reception to year 1. These difficulties are compounded in GRTF as they may not have attended a single school for any great length of time, therefore there is little information shared between settings and schools, especially if families move between local authorities. Given that children in England are more ethnically and culturally diverse than any other age group, inclusion in the early years is about ensuring that all children have access to a range of play and learning activities which meet their individual needs to enable them to reach their full potential.

Principles of inclusive practice

ACTIVITY 3

Begin to consider early years practice. What would you expect to see in an inclusive early years setting?

Cate et al. (2010) suggest that there are three elements which identify inclusive early years practice. These are: accessibility, participation and support. To extend this further, inclusive practice should also be enabling, that is it should enable all children to achieve their full potential (see Figure 7.1).

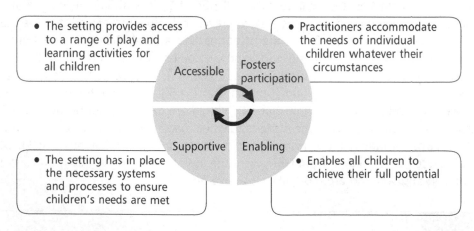

Figure 7.1 Inclusive early years practice

Adapted from Cate et al. (2010)

Inclusive practice depends not upon the child's ability to 'fit in' with the setting, rather it is dependent upon the attitude of practitioners within the setting, the practitioner's skills, knowledge and understanding of inclusion in its broadest sense and also upon the environment within the setting. Early years settings should have a welcoming atmosphere. Practitioners should be respectful of all children and their families, and accept and value individual differences between children irrespective of their learning ability, religion, culture or ethnic origin. Early years practitioners should welcome and be willing to work with all children, as Nutbrown (1996, p54) states:

> *not just children who are easy to work with, obliging, endearing, clean, pretty, articulate, capable, but every child – respecting them for who they are, respecting their language, their culture, their history, their family, their abilities, their needs, their name, their ways and their very essence.*

ACTIVITY 4

Return to the definition of inclusion which you wrote down earlier. Does your definition of inclusion reflect that inclusive early years practice respects and values all children, not just those with SEN and disabilities? If it doesn't, try to change what you have written to give a more comprehensive definition.

Inclusive practice is a result of the interplay between political and social influences which impact upon the way we, as practitioners, respond to individual differences between children. While there are legislative frameworks which govern how we should respond, in essence inclusive practice is dependent upon the individuals within settings, that is, it is our responsibility to ensure that all children are valued and treated with respect. As practitioners we should, as Ainscow (2007) suggests, examine our own assumptions to develop new ways of thinking to provide early years services which meet the needs of all children. As practitioners, we should be aware of our own prejudices and biases which we have learned, put these to one side and learn to respect and value diversity. Children from a very early age recognise differences. If we treat children differently or have negative attitudes towards children on the bases of our own prejudices this will have a profound impact upon how the child views him or herself.

ACTIVITY 5

Consider your own feelings and think how you would feel if you were treated differently or less favourably than those around you. Imagine how a child would feel, especially when perhaps they don't understand the reason behind the actions.

Inclusive practice: policy and legislation

In the UK it is unlawful to refuse children access to education on the basis of their gender, culture, religion, ethnicity, ability or physical disability. There is a plethora of policies and legislation relating to inclusion. However, much of it is specifically related to the inclusion of children with SEN and disabilities. We discussed at the beginning of this chapter that inclusion is about ensuring that *all* children have their individual needs met whatever their circumstances, so that they can achieve their full potential. The United Nations Charter for the Rights of Children (1989) which came into force in the UK in 1990 ensured that the world recognised that children have human rights too and acknowledges that every child has the right to education without discrimination. Table 7.1 identifies many of the policies and legislation which have guided inclusive practice, though the list is not exhaustive. As you can see from the table, inclusion it not a new concept but has been at the forefront of political discourse, that is it has been discussed in the political arena for many decades.

Table 7.1 Inclusive practice: policy and legislation

Education focus	Social focus
• Warnock Report (1978)	• UNCRC
• Education Acts 1981, 1993, 1996	• Children Act 1989
• Education Reform Act 1988	• Every Child Matters (2003) / ECM – Change for Children (2004)
• Education Act 1996	• Children Act 2004
• Disability Discrimination Acts 1995, 2005	• Common Assessment Framework (CAF) (2006)
• SENDA 2001	• Disability Discrimination Acts 1995, 2005
• SEN Code of Practice (2001)	• Children's Plan – Building Brighter Futures (2007)
• Education Act 2002	• Aiming High for Disabled Children (2007)
• Removing Barriers to Achievement (2004)	• 'Support for Families' Green Paper (2012)
• Warnock: Special Educational Needs: A New Look (2005)	• Equality Act 2010
• Children's Plan – Building Brighter Futures (2007)	
• Achievement for All (2008)	
• Bercow Report (2008)	
• Lamb Inquiry (2009)	
• Statutory Framework for the Early Years Foundation Stage (DfE, 2012b)	

As you can see from Table 7.1, the policies and legislation promoting inclusion have been divided into two areas, those which have an educational focus and those which have a broader social focus. For the purposes of this chapter we will focus our discussion on the Equality Act 2010 (HM Government, 2010) and the Statutory Framework for the Early Years Foundation Stage (EYFS) (DfE, 2012b).

The 2010 Equality Act (EA) is a single Act which replaces existing discrimination laws and came into force in October 2010. Within the EA it is acknowledged that every child has the right to access and receive their education without discrimination. The EA also acknowledges that children can be discriminated against directly or indirectly.

ACTIVITY 6

What do we mean by direct and indirect discrimination? Begin to consider early years practice: think of an example of direct and indirect discrimination within early years practice.

Direct discrimination occurs when a child is treated less favourably than their peers on the basis of their gender, culture, religion, ethnicity, ability or physical disability. This also includes discrimination against children on the basis their association, that is their relationship to or friendship with a child from any one of the categories mentioned.

CASE STUDY 1

Paul and Mahmood were best friends and attended their local nursery school. When at home with his family, Mahmood always spoke in Urdu and as a result Mahmood's spoken English was not very good and he had difficulty articulating his thoughts, although he appeared to understand what was being asked or discussed. Paul was very protective of Mahmood and would often speak on his behalf. Every day at story time, Mahmood would be taken out of the group to work on his spoken English. Paul was always asked to go with Mahmood because he was his friend.

After a week Paul's parents asked to speak to Paul's key worker, explaining that Paul was upset because he was asked to go with Mahmood every story time. Paul loved story time but didn't like to let Mahmood down therefore he didn't say anything to the practitioners. Paul's parents felt that he was being treated less favourably than his peers on the basis of his friendship with Mahmood.

Paul's keyworker explained that they hadn't realised that they were treating Paul less favourably and thought that because Paul didn't object he didn't mind going with Mahmood. During the discussion with Paul's parents the keyworker realised that not only was Paul being treated less favourably than his peers, they were also treating Mahmood less favourably by not letting him join in with story time, particularly as Mahmood could understand the story.

ACTIVITY 7

Begin to consider early years practice. In promoting inclusive practice should all children be treated the same? Think about the reasons for your answer.

If all children are treated the same, how can we ensure that the individual needs of all children are met? In reality we can't. Inclusion is not about treating everyone the same, it is about acknowledging differences between children and ensuring that despite their differences all children are given the opportunity to participate fully in play and learning activities to enable them to achieve their full potential. The EA identifies that 'indirect' discrimination occurs when, as a result of all children being treated the same, children with additional needs are disadvantaged compared to their peers.

ACTIVITY 8

Begin to consider early years practice. Think of a strategy that you could put in place to ensure that all children feel included and are able to contribute to discussions and activities.

CASE STUDY 2

Agata and her family are Polish; they came to live in the North East of England in June 2010. Agata's family wanted her to attend the local nursery school believing that this would help Agata to improve her English before she joined the reception class the following year. When at home the family spoke Polish, so when Agata first started the nursery she could not speak English very well, although she appeared to understand what was said.

It was customary that at the end of each session the children went into small discussion groups to talk about the activities they had done that morning. To ensure that Agata was fully involved in the discussions, the nursery practitioner would show examples of the activities which were available that morning. Agata was asked to select the activities she did and demonstrate to the other children what she made and so on. Initially, Agata would only confirm what she had made when prompted by the practitioner, but gradually as she gained more confidence in her ability to say what she had done, Agata began to extend her descriptions.

Let us now focus our attention on the Early Years Foundation Stage (EYFS) (DfE, 2012b). The EYFS is a statutory framework for all early years providers who are on the early years register, that is they have demonstrated to the Office for Standards in Education, Children's Services and Skills (Ofsted) that they can effectively deliver play and learning activities to ensure that all children learn and develop well and are kept safe and healthy. The EYFS was first introduced in 2007 and, as with all government initiatives, was reviewed in 2011 (DfE, 2011a). The revised EYFS came into force in September 2012 and sets out the standards which all early years providers must meet to ensure that children achieve the best that they can.

The EYFS promotes inclusive practice by ensuring that all children have access to learning and development activities which meet their individual needs and interests and by ensuring that every child is supported and fully included in the setting. The EYFS identifies four principles (see Table 7.2) which should influence early years practice – all four principles foster and promote inclusive practice.

Table 7.2 EYFS guiding principles

EYFS principles	Influences inclusive practice by ensuring that:
Every Child Is a Unique Child	Every child is constantly learning and can be resilient, capable, confident and self-assured irrespective of their age, race, culture, religion, gender, language.
Positive Relationship	All children learn to be independent and strong through positive relationships with both adults and other children.
Enabling Environments	All children are able to access experiences which respond to their individual needs. Promote positive relationships with parents and carers.
Acknowledges Differences in Learning and Development	Education and care enables children to develop and learn in different ways and at different times, including those with SEN or disability.

Adapted from DfE (2012b, p3)

In addition to the learning and development requirements, Section 3 of the EYFS outlines the Safeguarding and Welfare Requirements (SWR) which are designed to ensure that settings welcome all children and that they are kept safe. The SWR aim to ensure that practitioners take into account the holistic needs of children, not just their educational needs. For example, Section 3.45 states that *providers must record and act on information from parents and carers about a child's dietary needs.*

This ensures that where a child has a restricted diet, for example children from strict Hindu families are not allowed to eat meat, their dietary requirements are met and they are given a nutritionally balanced meal. Additionally, in line with the Disability and Discrimination Act 2005, early years providers must ensure that *so far as is reasonable, the facilities, equipment and access to the premises are suitable for children with disabilities* (DfE, 2012b, p24).

To further support inclusive early years practice Section 3.66 of the SWR requires all early years providers to have and implement a policy and procedures which promote equality of opportunity for all children. Providers must also have effective systems to review, monitor and evaluate the effectiveness of inclusive practices, to ensure that practitioners promote and value diversity and difference within their setting.

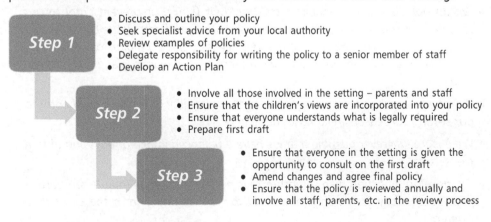

Step 1
- Discuss and outline your policy
- Seek specialist advice from your local authority
- Review examples of policies
- Delegate responsibility for writing the policy to a senior member of staff
- Develop an Action Plan

Step 2
- Involve all those involved in the setting – parents and staff
- Ensure that the children's views are incorporated into your policy
- Ensure that everyone understands what is legally required
- Prepare first draft

Step 3
- Ensure that everyone in the setting is given the opportunity to consult on the first draft
- Amend changes and agree final policy
- Ensure that the policy is reviewed annually and involve all staff, parents, etc. in the review process

Figure 7.2 Three steps to developing and monitoring your early years equality and diversity policy

ACTIVITY 9

Begin to consider early years practice. What do you think an Equality and Diversity Policy should include? Make a list of points to consider.

When developing an equality and diversity policy practitioners should ensure that the policy:

- includes a mission statement which states that the setting is committed to promoting anti-discriminatory practice for all children and their families;
- outlines the aims of the policy;
- sets out the legal framework underpinning the policy;
- sets out the admissions policy to ensure that no child or family will be refused a place on the grounds of their religion, culture, ethnicity, gender, social background or disability;
- outlines the recruitment process to ensure that the diversity of staff reflects the local community;
- outlines how the management will challenge discrimination within the setting.

CASE STUDY 3

Extract from Little Teds Equality and Diversity Policy: Admissions:

- *Our setting is open to all members of the community.*

- *We advertise our service widely.*

- *We reflect the diversity of our society in our publicity and promotional materials.*

- *We provide information in clear, concise language, whether in spoken or written form.*

- *We provide information in as many languages as possible.*

- *We base our admissions policy on a fair system.*

- *We ensure that all parents are made aware of our equal opportunities policy.*

- *We do not discriminate against a child or their family, or prevent entry to our setting, on the basis of a protected characteristic as defined by the Equalities Act 2010. These are: disability, race, gender reassignment, religion or belief, sex, sexual orientation, age, pregnancy and maternity, and marriage and civil partnership.*

- *We do not discriminate against a child with a disability or refuse a child entry to our setting for reasons relating to disability.*

- *We ensure wherever possible that we have a balanced intake of boys and girls in the setting.*

- *We develop an action plan to ensure that people with impairments can participate successfully in the services offered by the setting and in the curriculum offered.*

CASE STUDY 3 *continued*

- *We take action against any discriminatory behaviour by staff or parents whether by:*
  - *Direct discrimination – someone is treated less favourably because of a protected characteristic, e.g. preventing families of some racial groups from using the service;*
  - *Indirect discrimination – someone is affected unfavourably by a general policy, e.g. children must only speak English in the setting;*
  - *Association – discriminating against someone who is associated with a person with a protected characteristic, e.g. behaving unfavourably to someone who is married to a person from a different cultural background; or*
  - *Perception – discrimination on the basis that it is thought someone has a protected characteristic, e.g. assuming someone is gay because of their mannerisms or how they speak.*
  - *Displaying of openly discriminatory and possibly offensive materials, name calling or threatening behaviour are unacceptable on or around the premises and will be dealt with in the strongest manner.*

We have discussed two examples of legislation and statutory guidance which have a profound impact on the way in which early years services are delivered. Both the EA and EYFS reflect the government's commitment to ensure that children and their families are protected against discrimination, that they are given every opportunity to participate fully in society and that they have access to a fair and equitable education which enables all children to reach their full potential. The UNESCO (1994, p11) World Salamanca Statement stipulates that:

> *Inclusion and participation are essential to human dignity and to the enjoyment and exercise of human rights. Within the field of education this is reflected in the development of strategies that seek to bring a genuine equalisation of opportunity.*

As we discussed earlier, inclusive practice depends not upon the children's ability to 'fit in' with the setting, rather it is dependent upon the attitude of practitioners, therefore as early years practitioners we must ensure that the service we provide is fully inclusive and respects and values diversity irrespective of our own values and beliefs.

From segregation to full inclusion

At the beginning of this chapter, we acknowledged that all children have the right to be educated together and without discrimination. However, this has not always been the case. At the beginning of the twentieth century, if a child's needs could not be met within schools, these children were often described as being 'un-educable'. However, the introduction of the Education (Handicapped Children) Act 1970 resulted in the construction of many special schools which those children with disabilities or special educational needs attended. As a result children with SEN or disabilities were segregated from children who attended mainstream schools. *Segregation* can also occur within a mainstream school.

ACTIVITY 10

Reflecting on your own experiences of school, give an example when children have been segregated from other pupils. How do you think that child would feel when removed from the classroom?

Segregation within a mainstream school is the act of taking children out of their class to be taught separately. An example of this is taking children who have English as an additional language (EAL) out of their class to teach them English with children who have similar needs. Historically, removing children from their peers to teach English was common practice; however, this is not so much the case today. The setting, whether that is a nursery or reception class, is a social learning space therefore children whose first language is not English should be provided with opportunities to participate in meaningful conversations with both adults and other children. Children learn best when they feel safe and secure and have a sense of belonging. Segregating children from their peers does not promote inclusive practices irrespective of how well intentioned the reasons are for this.

In an attempt to provide a more inclusive educational system, specialist resource units were established on the premises of mainstream schools. This saw a shift in focus from segregation to *integration*. Ainscow (1999) suggests that integration is about making a limited number of additional arrangements for individual pupils with SEN in schools. Ainscow (1999) further suggests that the focus of integration is on the process of assimilation, that is integration enables the child to 'fit in' with the school. However, as we discussed earlier, inclusion is not about the child's ability to 'fit in'.

CASE STUDY 4

Cherry Tree Primary School

Christopher was hearing impaired and attended Cherry Tree Primary School nursery class. Attached to the school was a specialist unit for hearing-impaired children. The unit was staffed by a specialist teacher for the hearing-impaired and support staff.

Every day, a member of staff from the 'unit' would collect Christopher from the nursery and take him to the unit for small-group work with other hearing-impaired children. The staff would work with Christopher to reinforce topics discussed in the nursery.

At times Christopher was reluctant to leave his friends or the activity he was doing and often resented having to go to the unit.

Christopher's parents moved to the area specifically so that Christopher could attend the same school as his elder brother. Having a specialist unit for hearing impaired children on the school premises enabled Christopher to 'fit in' with the school.

ACTIVITY *11*

Consider to what extent you think Cherry Tree School is providing inclusive education?

A fully inclusive school or early years setting is one which adapts to the needs of all children and ensures that *all* children have their individual needs met whatever their circumstances so that they can achieve their full potential. Therefore, inclusion is concerned with the process of *accommodation*, that is the onus is upon the school to change and adapt to be responsive to the needs of all children. Children are entitled to be educated together, not just together in the same school, but in the same class as their peers. In Case Study 4 above, Christopher was removed from his peers to receive specialist support. In a fully inclusive environment, the specialist teacher and support staff would work with Christopher alongside his peers in the normal classroom environment.

ACTIVITY *12*

Begin to consider early years practice. Is fully inclusive practice really achievable?

Inclusion does not just occur naturally – inclusion is a process based upon reflection. A fully inclusive early years setting is one in which practitioners continually reflect upon their practice to overcome barriers which prevent children from participating fully in play and learning activities. Practitioners view each child as unique, nurturing their learning and development to ensure that they achieve their full potential. In reality, it may be appropriate to temporarily remove a child from the normal classroom or setting environment to receive specialist teaching. However, the overarching aim of inclusive practice is to ensure that all children are educated with their peers in the same class.

Theoretical frameworks to support inclusion

The focus of our next discussion is upon theoretical frameworks which help aid our understanding of inclusion specifically in relation to children who have disabilities and SEN. The three frameworks or models to be discussed illustrate how, over time, explanations of inclusion have developed to foster a more inclusive educational system.

The psycho-medical model

The psycho-medical model (PMM) as described by Skidmore (1996) focuses upon the individual differences between children which are caused by specific disabilities or medical conditions. Within the PMM comparisons are made between the performance of children with disabilities or SEN and children of a similar age. When applied to inclusive early years practice, within the PMM it is assumed that if children cannot perform as well as other children of a similar age it is because of their disability or condition rather than the ability of practitioners to accommodate the child's needs. If a child who, by virtue of their disability, was unable to participate in education in a mainstream school they would, in all probability, be educated in a special school or special resource unit, that is they would be segregated from their peers.

ACTIVITY 13

Begin to consider early years practice. Is it right to assume that all children who have a disability have a learning difficulty?

Not all children who have a disability have learning difficulties. For example, children with visual impairments do not necessarily have a learning difficulty, therefore it does not seem appropriate to exclude these children from mainstream education purely on the basis of their visual impairment. One of the weaknesses associated with the PMM of explanation is that it focuses on what the child cannot do compared to children of a similar age, rather than what the child can do or could do if the correct level of support was available. Within the PMM a child's education is determined to some extent by professionals in the diagnosis of their medical condition. For example, a child who has a visual impairment will be educated in a school which caters for children who have a visual impairment. Therefore it can be argued that children who have disabilities are being discriminated against. To iterate, the United Nations Charter for the Rights of Children (UNCRC, 1998) advocates that children have human rights too and acknowledges that every child has the right to education without discrimination.

The social model of disability

In contrast to the PMM, the social model of disability (SMD) as described by Hughes and Patterson (1997) advocates that it is the attitudes of those within society and the restrictions of the environment that disadvantage those with disabilities rather than the disability itself. Subsequently, the barriers encountered to overcome these disadvantages prevent individuals from being fully included in society. Earlier in the chapter we acknowledged that inclusive early years practice was dependent upon the attitude of practitioners within the setting, the practitioners' skills, knowledge and understanding of inclusion, and also upon the environment within the setting. Within the SMD it can be assumed that if practitioners have a positive attitude and, in accordance with the legislation, i.e. Special Educational Needs and Disability Act 2001, make reasonable adjustments to buildings and to the learning environment to remove barriers to inclusion then all children can have access to education in a mainstream school or setting.

ACTIVITY 14

Begin to consider early years practice. Do you think that it would be reasonable or practical to educate all children who have disabilities or learning difficulties in a mainstream school? Can you give an example to demonstrate you view?

Rights-based model of disability

To reiterate, the UNCRC (1989) which came into force in the UK in 1990, ensured that the world recognised that children have human rights too and acknowledges that every child has the right to education without discrimination. The rights-based model (RBM) (Kenworthy and Whittaker, 2000) is based upon this recognition and is driven by political aspirations for a fully inclusive education system, a system in which no child, irrespective of their gender, culture, religion, ethnicity, ability or physical disability, is discriminated against. The RBM suggests that it is society's structures, values and beliefs which hinder inclusion and advocates that where necessary legislation should be used to ensure that discrimination does not occur. Within the RBM all schools and early years settings would be fully inclusive and there would be no need for segregation within education.

ACTIVITY 15

Warnock (2005, p37) states that inclusion is not a matter of where you are geographically, but of where you belong.

To what extent do you agree or disagree with this statement?

CASE STUDY 5

Christopher has cerebral palsy and as a result has a curvature of the spine. He also has epilepsy and difficulty in speaking. He walks with the aid of a walking frame. Christopher does not have any specific learning difficulties.

Christopher's parents fought to have him educated in mainstream education. He enjoyed primary school where the children and staff were very accommodating of his needs. However, at the age of 13 Christopher attended his local comprehensive school. Christopher had reservations about going to the school because he knew he would be ridiculed by the older children. However, Christopher's parents insisted that he went.

When Christopher left school he later enrolled at the local college to study an introductory course in teaching as he wanted to teach ICT. During his course Christopher disclosed to his tutor that he *hated going to comprehensive school, and had wished that his parents had allowed him to attend a nearby special school, as he never felt that he 'fitted in' with the school, and was taunted by some of the other pupils.*

Every effort should be made to ensure that all children receive their education without discrimination, and *should wherever possible receive their education in a mainstream school* (DfEE, 1997, p44). However, in reality it is not always appropriate for all children to be educated in mainstream school. If a child has very severe and complex disabilities or learning difficulties it is often not practical or realistic to expect that these children should be educated in mainstream school, therefore in these circumstances it is in the best interests of the child to be educated in a special school. Two important factors which should be taken into consideration when determining where a child receives their education are the views and opinions of the child and parents.

Promoting and maintaining partnership with parents

When discussing inclusive early years practice, it was concluded that inclusion is about ensuring that all children and their families feel valued and supported. The discussion which follows will focus upon inclusive practice which welcomes and values partnerships with parents. The CWDC (2010, p78) refers to parents as mothers, fathers, legal guardians and primary carers of looked-after children, that is children who are being looked after either by foster carers or in residential homes. Working in partnership with parents is not an option; early years practitioners have a legal obligation to promote, foster and maintain positive working relations with parents. Outlined below is an overview of the various legal frameworks which place a statutory obligation on all early years practitioners to work in partnership with parents.

- The Warnock Report (1978) recognised the importance of partnership with parents.
- The Education Act 1981 placed new power with parents of children with SEN.
- The Children Act 1989 introduced the concept of parental responsibility.
- DfES (2001): Special Educational Needs Code of Practice.
- DFES (2004): Every Child Matters: Change for Children emphasised the importance of working in partnership with parents, children and young people.
- The Children Act 2004 sets out the legal responsibility placed on LAs/schools and services to work in partnership with parents, children and young people.
- The Childcare Act 2006 requires all settings, schools and LAs to provide information to parents outlining the services available to children and their families.
- DfE (2012b) Statutory Framework for the Early Years Foundation Stage stipulates that practitioners should work in partnership with parents and carers.

Working in partnership with parents will instil a sense of value and make them feel respected and more confident to support their children's learning at home. Swick (2004) identified that parents expected practitioners to care about them and their children, be respectful and value their contribution to children's learning and involve them in their child's learning. Above all else parents wanted a relationship which was based on two-way communication.

ACTIVITY 16

Begin to consider early years practice. How could you encourage parents to be involved in children's learning?

CASE STUDY 6

A celebration of light

The nursery practitioners were preparing for Christmas, and during their discussions with the children Ethan stated that *he didn't celebrate Christmas like we do*. Ethan was Jewish. The nursery practitioners thought it would be a good idea to ask Ethan's mum if she could come into the nursery and talk to the children about Hanukkah, which is a festival celebrated by Jewish families in November or December. The festival involves lighting one candle a day on the hanukkiah (an eight-stemmed candelabrum). During this festival the children play traditional Jewish games. Ethan's mum came into nursery and told the children about Hanukkah and demonstrated how they lit the hanukkiah. Ethan was also involved and showed the children how to play a game using the dreidel, which resembles a spinning top. Ethan and his mum then taught the children the dreidel song.

It was a wonderful experience for the children, but more importantly it made Ethan and his family feel valued and respected.

ACTIVITY 17

Begin to consider early years practice. How do you think practitioners can foster and maintain effective working relationships with parents?

Fostering and promoting positive relationships with parents: points to consider

Figure 7.3 outlines the points to consider when fostering and promoting positive relationships with parents.

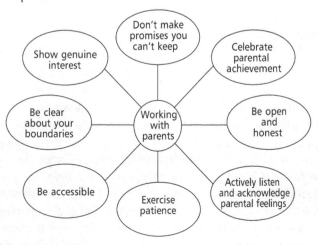

Figure 7.3 Working with parents

Adapted from Ward (2009)

Skills and knowledge required to work with children and families

As is customary throughout this book, consider the skills and knowledge required to work with children and families, reflect upon your own skills and knowledge, and identify those which you need to develop further. The template presented in Table 7.3 outlines the skills and knowledge required for working with children and families identified in the Common Core of Skills and Knowledge (CWDC, 2010).

Table 7.3 Personal development plan

Working with children and families	What do I need to learn?	How will this be achieved?	Resources required	Evidence of achievement	Target date
Skills: Good communication skills Listening and building empathy Summarising and explaining **Knowledge:** How to consult and engage Where to obtain sources of information The importance of respect					

CHAPTER SUMMARY

Throughout this chapter we have explored the concept of inclusion, acknowledging that inclusion in early years practice is about ensuring that all children, irrespective of their learning ability, religion, culture or ethnic origin, have access to play and learning activities which enable them to achieve their full potential. The process of inclusion is based upon reflective practice, and as practitioners we must continually strive to ensure that every child, whatever their circumstances, feels included, respected and valued. The three theoretical frameworks discussed outline how, over time, there has been a shift in focus from segregation to the provision of a more inclusive environment. Promoting and fostering an inclusive environment is both challenging and rewarding. As early years practitioners it is our responsibility to endeavour to remove any barriers to learning and development to ensure that children receive their education without discrimination.

Self-assessment questions

1. What is the difference between the following: segregation, integration and full inclusion?
2. Identify one possible weakness within each of the three theoretical frameworks discussed.
3. What are the four elements of inclusive practice discussed?

FURTHER READING

Cook, T (2004) Starting where we can: using action research to develop inclusive practice, *International Journal of Early Years Education*, 12 (1): 3–15.

Rogers, A and Wilmot, E (2011) *Inclusion and Diversity in the Early Years (Early Childhood Essentials)*. London: Practical Pre-school Books.

Rogers, C (2007) Experiencing an 'inclusive' education: parents and their children with 'Special Educational Needs', *British Journal of Sociology of Education*, 28 (1): 55–68.

Wilkin, A, Berrington, C, White, R, Martin, K, Foster, B, Kinder, K and Rutt, S (2010) *Improving outcomes for Gypsy Roma, Traveller Pupils: Final Report*. London: DCSF.

8 Ensuring safe practice
Martin Harmer

Reading through this chapter will help you to:

- consider ways to encourage children's own active contribution to keeping themselves safe;

- gain confidence in applying procedures to situations where concerns exist;

- explore how best to communicate with parents and other professionals about such issues;

- understand your contribution to wider multi-agency processes;

- extend your understanding of how to help children with their reactions after abuse;

- identify areas for development to be included in your personal development action plan.

Key trends: are children safer?

Recent cases within early years settings illustrate where a culture was allowed to develop which made challenging inappropriate behaviour by staff difficult, e.g. the taking and sharing of indecent images of children at Little Teds Nursery (Plymouth SCB, 2010), and a teacher committing 36 sexual offences against children as young as six at a first school (North Somerset SCB, 2012).

Similarly, inquiries into individual children's deaths due to parental abuse and neglect – such as the physical abuse/extreme malnourishment experienced by Khyra Ishaq (Birmingham CB, 2010) – could be interpreted as a continuing failure of the system for safeguarding children.

ACTIVITY 1

Read the Executive Summary of the Serious Case Review on Sexual Abuse at the School in Somerset at: **www.northsomersetlscb.org.uk/uploads/files/282.pdf**.

What actions might have been taken to stop this earlier?

Despite these individual cases, however, there are reasons for optimism:

- Summary incidence studies based on serious case reviews show deaths as a result of abuse have fallen from 174 in 2008–9 to 90 in 2009–10 (Ofsted, 2010). Further supporting evidence estimates a long-term reduction of abuse-related deaths of around 67 per cent in England and Wales between 1974 and 2006/2008 (Pritchard and Williams, 2010; Sidebotham et al., 2011).

- Two studies looking at the prevalence of abuse generally, undertaken ten years apart by the NSPCC (Cawson et al., 2000; Radford et al., 2011), offer the strongest evidence in the UK, with large samples of respondents and strong research design allowing meaningful comparisons over this period. These comparisons show large reductions in verbal and physical abuse, small reductions in sexual abuse, but no change in levels of neglect (Radford et al., 2011).
- We have stronger evidence of 'what works' in the prevention and treatment of some types of abuse, detailed later in this chapter.

Context: policy directions 1990–2010

The Children Act 1989 reaffirmed two key duties on local authorities. The duty to investigate possible significant harm reworded a previous duty. But the 1989 Act established a stronger preventative duty than its predecessor to provide services for children 'in need' who were 'unlikely to achieve/maintain a reasonable standard of health or development' without them. During the 1990s, despite this change, the reactive, investigative approach continued to be prioritised over preventative work, and this trend was evidenced by a series of studies summarised in *Messages from Research* (DoH, 1995). The key message was that a single incident of abuse is seldom as concerning (with some severe exceptions) as ongoing 'low warmth/high criticism' environments which undermine children's well-being on a daily basis. The suggested solution was to undertake fewer investigations, redirecting resources more towards preventative work. This was known as the 'refocusing' debate.

This refocusing of resources towards prevention and longer-term support was strengthened under successive Labour governments (1997–2010). It was reflected in the provisions of the Children Act 2004 – with the introduction of the Common Assessment Framework (CAF) to integrate planned support for families where children were 'in need', and growth in the numbers of Sure Start Children's Centres to act as community supports for young families. Changes of terminology are often important, and the change from the narrow focus on 'child protection' to the wider concept of 'safeguarding' underlines this shift in approach. Safeguarding was now recognised to be required at three different levels: 'universal safeguarding' to keep all children safe (for example, safe play areas, internet safety); 'targeted safeguarding' where specific support is given to certain more vulnerable groups (e.g. children with special needs and disabilities, children whose parents use drugs) in order to prevent harm; and 'responsive safeguarding' where timely help and intervention is provided for children who have suffered harm.

This wider focus on prevention has continued through various reports (e.g. DCSF, 2008c) and pilot implementations of the 'Think Family' initiatives, the Family Nurse Partnership and other early intervention funding to local authorities under the Labour government. The Early Intervention Grant initially continued under the Coalition, with reduced funding but some greater flexibility. However, this has since been reduced further in order to fund the free places for disadvantaged two year olds (Jozwiak, 2012). In contrast to this, further reports have continued to emphasise the long-term savings to be made from an early support approach (e.g. C4EO and WAVE Trust, 2010; Allen, 2011b) and to make policy recommendations to further its development. The Coalition government's responses are discussed later.

Alongside greater use of preventative approaches has been a much stronger emphasis on multi-agency working, partly in response to the continued findings of serious case reviews about ineffective communication (Sinclair and Bullock, 2002; Ofsted, 2010), but also so that assessment of and support for families is better co-ordinated. The strengthened role of the Local Safeguarding Children Boards to plan and monitor service delivery in their areas that became law under the Children Act 2004 helps this process, as does the CAF and the Common Core of Skills discussed in Chapter 2. Proposals for web-based information sharing on children, which became known as Contact Point, were eventually scrapped by the Coalition after technical problems and data security concerns, but would have helped to identify which professionals were actively in contact with a particular child. Partly replacing this by 2015 is a national database announced for the NHS to allow the sharing of child protection concerns between hospitals.

A final key theme which has developed over the last decade has been that of safe-guarding being 'everyone's responsibility' and not something that can be left to social workers, health professionals and the police. Every Child Matters stated this in regard to securing all of the 'five outcomes': *Families, communities, government, public services, voluntary organisations, business, the media and others have a crucial part to play in valuing children, protecting them, promoting their interests and listening to their views* (Chief Secretary to the Treasury, 2003, p14), a sentiment repeated in the Staying Safe Action Plan (DCSF, 2008c), and well summarised by the NSPCC: *All adults must be alert to the warning signs, all children given the opportunities and confidence to ask for help* (NSPCC, 2011, p4).

Early years professionals have a crucially important role here in:

- listening to and valuing children in order to build their confidence;

- protecting them by being alert to warning signs and taking correct and timely action to offer early help or referral where necessary;

- promoting their interests in meetings with parents and professionals where decisions are made;

- supporting parents and carers in the task of safeguarding;

- caring for children who have experienced the effects of abuse and neglect.

We will return to consider future policy directions later, but for now let us further develop our understanding of the knowledge and skills required to effectively take on our part of the joint responsibility we share for safeguarding children.

Universal safeguarding: workforce issues and setting culture

Since their introduction and in their current version, the EYFS Safeguarding and Welfare Requirements (DfE, 2012b) require settings to meet a range of safety issues. These detail a number of physical and health requirements such as the safety and security of buildings and equipment, risk assessments, preventing infection, administering medicines and obtaining emergency medical treatment. They also require settings to ensure children's emotional well-being through managing behaviour appropriately and assigning each child a 'key person'.

Settings need to create and effectively implement their own safeguarding policy, communicated with parents. One practitioner needs to act as the Designated Lead Person with responsibility for safeguarding. They need to ensure that staff understand the policy and are trained to recognise signs/symptoms of abuse and neglect and know how to implement procedures.

In terms of safe recruitment, settings need to ensure staff are suitable, with appropriate training and knowledge. The document *Safeguarding Children and Safer Recruitment in Education* (DfES, 2006b, but currently being considered for review) offers detailed guidance on how to deter unsuitable applicants by ensuring the advert, job description, person specification and information packs stress the organisation's commitment to safeguarding. Good practice suggested here requires the use of application forms and not CVs so that questions cannot easily be avoided or gaps in employment dates hidden. References must be gathered directly from the referee, prompting for information with specific questions. One member of the interview panel should have attended safer recruitment training, and rather than using hypothetical questions, value-based interviewing techniques (Erooga, 2009) allow interviewers to probe for detailed examples of real past experiences (e.g. 'Tell us about a time when you had to deal with a delicate situation with a parent? What did you do/say?').

Successful candidates need to prove their identity and qualifications, apply for an enhanced DBS check with the Disclosure and Barring Service (from December 2012). This includes the existing enhanced CRB check and a check against the list of people barred from working with children or vulnerable adults. Any new allegations against staff must be passed to the LADO (Local Authority Designated Officer) and to Ofsted. If a staff member is found to have harmed or posed a risk of harm to a child the Disclosure and Barring Service must be notified.

Key additions to setting safeguarding practices under the Safeguarding and Welfare Requirements include that information should be shared on the types of adult behaviour which may indicate a risk to children, that the setting's safeguarding policy must give guidance on appropriate use of mobile phones and cameras, and that staff supervision is provided in order to train staff, provide mutual support and enable confidential discussion of sensitive issues. These changes are influenced by the findings of the Little Teds case where a member of staff used her mobile phone to take indecent photographs of children in the toilet area, then shared them over the internet. While the Serious Case Review (Plymouth SCB, 2010) concluded this risk could not easily have been predicted, the environment within Little Teds was con-ducive to abuse – with recruitment procedures not being followed, alliances being allowed to form among staff, and no clear procedures for staff on action to take if they had concerns within the workplace.

Managers and teams need to regularly review their own interactions and team phi-losophy in order to achieve an open and supportive emotional environment for staff, children and parents. One simple and inspiring philosophy, requiring attention and emotional bravery to achieve in practice, is 'Honest open and truthful communication with everyone' (Rushforth, 2012, p75). A recent study of best practice in safeguarding (Mortimer et al., 2012) is relevant to primary schools and early years settings. It again stresses the importance of a comprehensive safeguarding philosophy expressed through such things as the visibility of senior staff, a 'zero threshold' where any member of staff can raise even small concerns, and having a range of 'listening systems' such as 'teachers' times to talk', worry boxes, circle time and circles of friends. A companion document (Office of the Children's Commissioner, 2012) includes a helpful self-assessment and development plan guide for settings.

Universal safeguarding: developing resilience in children

The concept of resilience – the ability to cope with trauma or adversity – is particularly important for children experiencing difficult situations, but is beneficial for all chil-dren. Three sets of factors interact to influence resilience: a child's individual coping strategies and problem-solving skills; their family; and other support systems in their environment such as early years settings and schools (Masten et al., 1990; Cefai, 2008).

Adults in such settings can have a positive effect on this process by teaching coping strategies, but can also provide positive adult/child relationships that may be missing elsewhere. Many of the actions which support resilience are what most practitioners do naturally: showing care and concern, offering routine and consistent discipline, and building children's trust by keeping promises. Behaviour management needs to emphasise a positive approach – giving attention to and encouragement for what children do well so that it focuses on their strengths. Other actions include showing respect for the child's experience through active listening and empathy, and enabling the child to communicate about their feelings – the use of puppets and persona dolls being particularly helpful here. Allowing children to make choices (particularly about bodily contact), possibly by presenting a range of reasonable alternatives rather than a completely open choice, gives children more control. Encouraging friendships, helping children develop skills for making and maintaining friendships and tactics for resolving disagreements have been found to be very important too. Telling stories of survival in the face of challenge or adversity can teach skills and create a sense of optimism. Many children's stories naturally have such storylines (*Elmer*, *Matilda*, *The Hobbit*) but specific ones exist which deal with abusive situations (*Rosy and Jack*, *Your Body Belongs to You*) and help children understand how to stay safer.

Attempts to deliberately teach resilience include the UK Resilience Programme, piloted with year 7 children. Its aims were to promote more optimistic thinking, coping skills and social problem-solving in children to buffer them against anxiety and depression. Results showed significant but fairly short-lived improvements which faded by the two-year follow-up (Challen et al., 2011). In an attempt to counteract this tendency a 'spiral curriculum' approach has been used in other initiatives – where the skills are 'revisited' at different levels of development throughout a child's education – and this was the approach used in the Primary SEAL (Social and Emotional Aspects of Learning) programme, aimed at helping young children to manage their feelings, develop empathy and social skills, plan and problem-solve. PATHS (Promoting Alternative Thinking Strategies) covers similar ground, has material specifically for the pre-school level (Channing Bete, 2012) and has better evidence of effectiveness (Zins et al., 2004). It is used by several local authorities in the UK, including Birmingham. Other pro-grammes exist that attempt to teach skills for staying safe (Kidscape, 2007), including running away, yelling, telling and not keeping secrets, but this may be more relevant to 7–8 year olds and upwards. For younger ages some interesting ideas on delivering these skills in non-threatening ways as part of circle time are developed in *Ring of Confidence* (Vine and Todd, 2005).

Targeted safeguarding: recognition of possible harm

Detailed discussion of the recognition of the signs and symptoms of possible abuse and neglect is beyond the scope of this chapter, but see the NSPCC Core Info series and the Jigsaw entry in the references section.

Often, though, practitioners are aware of the signs but either fail to recognise them or fail to take action as a result. This can be due to an inbuilt resistance to accepting disturbing information designed to protect us from anxiety. Psychodynamic theory has long recognised repression ('I'm not seeing this') and rationalisation ('there must be some innocent explanation') as part of this process. It could though simply be that we are unaware of events outside our current focus of attention, described as the 'illusion of attention' by Chabris and Simons (2010a, 2010b) and demonstrated in their selective attention experiments.

ACTIVITY 2

Watch the Selective Attention Test: **http://bit.ly/U2jQHS**

What did you see? Then visit the link given in the reference list to find out more about the results.

Chabris and Simons also discuss 'change blindness' where we fail to see changes in detail over time. Awareness of these processes may guard against any 'smugness of hindsight' when reading Serious Case Reviews, and also help us understand non-abusing parents who say they weren't aware of what was happening. More importantly for practice, awareness can prompt us to at least check (have I missed anything?), and ensure that supervision and team discussions on children are prioritised, as sharing perceptions will help to counteract this tendency. Good record-keeping that allows patterns to be identified also becomes more important.

Obstacles to action are usually due to self-doubt and the internal thoughts we all have at such moments, most especially: 'what if I'm wrong?' Again, this can be helped by following procedures and sharing concerns with your Designated Lead Person.

The Safeguarding and Welfare Requirements no longer advise settings to follow the guidance given in *What to Do If You Are Worried a Child Is Being Abused – Summary* (DfES, 2006a) when they have concerns. The only reference is to 'Working Together to Safeguard Children'. This document is currently being rewritten, but the draft issued for consultation (WorkingTogetherOnline, 2012) contains no real detail to guide early years practitioners in how to talk with the child, how to discuss safeguarding issues with parents, how to request their consent to share information, or what actions to take to confirm a referral. Once the new 'Working Together' document is finalised it may be the government's intention not to replace the 'What to Do' guidance. Nevertheless, it remains good advice, and informs this section.

Obviously careful consideration of the facts – any injuries to the child, changed behaviour, something they or someone else has said, atypical parent/child interaction – needs to be undertaken to evaluate if you have sufficient evidence to take further action.

CASE STUDY 1

You are key person to Lily, aged three, at a nursery attached to a children's centre. Lily's father, Samuel, was recently made redundant. Lily has missed some sessions during the last two weeks, and when you rang home Samuel was angry, accusing you of sticking your nose into family business but saying she'd be in the next day. When Lily returns you notice two bruises on her left thigh which could be partial hand-prints. You ask Lily quite naturally about the injuries – 'they look sore, what happened?' – but she simply shakes her head and walks off. You quite rightly accept this response without further questioning. You inform the Designated Lead Person (the nursery manager here) of your concerns, and discuss together what to do next – deciding to ask the parents when they collect Lily shortly. Meanwhile the nursery manager confidentially asks the Children's Centre manager if they are aware of anything as Lily's mother, Davina, attends parents' groups there. Davina has expressed concerns to staff at the children's centre about Samuel's recent heavy drinking.

CASE STUDY 1 *continued*

It is Davina who collects Lily. When the nursery manager explains about the marks and asks if she knows what happened she becomes very frightened. When you explain that you understand that she wants the best for Lily and ask for her consent to inform Children's Social Care, she refuses and storms out.

Consider actions you might then take.

- Seek advice from Children's Social Care without identifying the family. They advise referral, and clarify that parents' consent is not necessary in this case (see Activity 3 below) where there is possible 'significant harm'.

- Formally refer your concerns to Children's Social Care, giving details and family information.

- Record factually the bruises seen and the question to Lily and how she responded, the discussion with Davina and what actions were then taken/decisions made (within 24 hours).

- Confirm your concerns in writing to Children's Social Care within 48 hours.

- Contact them again if you receive no acknowledgement within three days.

ACTIVITY 3

In Case Study 1 above, Children's Social Care advise that parental consent is unnecessary prior to referral. What circumstances are specifically mentioned in the 'Information Sharing' guidance (DCSF, 2008d) as being exceptions to needing to seek parental consent?

Now compare your answer to the suggested one at the end of this chapter.

When evaluating concerns observation of child/parent interaction can be very informative. Intuitively we recognise when a relationship between parent and child is 'secure' – when parents generally respond to their children's communications and meet their needs, and they enjoy being reunited at the end of the day. The parent offers and the child readily accepts comfort, and there are patterns of mutual responses.

But how can we back up this same intuition where we sense something wrong in the parent/child interaction? Theory would suggest that 'disorganised attachment' shown by the child and low levels of the skills of 'mentalisation' or 'reflective function' shown by the parent (Shemmings et al., 2012) would be indicators of concern. Estimates suggest that 10–15 per cent of children exhibit this kind of behaviour (Bakermans-Kranenberg et al., 2005), but that it is a temporary response to threat (natural disaster, abuse). Once a threat recedes 'disorganised' behaviours resolve into one of the three known styles of attachment (Ainsworth et al., 1978). Disorganised attachment is not related to children having special needs (van IJzendoorn, 1999). The two factors most closely associated with disorganised attachment in children are unresolved loss and trauma in the parent, and low levels of 'mentalisation' or 'reflective function'.

Unresolved loss and trauma may result in memories being triggered in the parent while with the child, so they may defend themselves by avoiding taking care of the child, or they may show contradictory behaviour between what they know they should do (respond to the child) and their unconscious emotional reaction (pulling away).

Low mentalisation/reflective function refers to difficulties that some parents experience in separating out what is happening within themselves as different from what is happening in the child – for example, if the parent is not hungry, they cannot understand that the child may be (Shemmings et al., 2012). They respond to their child on the basis of their own needs, and can therefore be intrusive or inappropriate (being very angry in response to some minor accident, demanding shows of sexualised affection). The child's actions may even be interpreted as targeted at the parent deliberately, e.g. 'he's thrown a tantrum in the supermarket to show me up as a bad parent'.

Typical reactions you might observe which suggest disorganised attachment are presented in Table 8.1.

Table 8.1 Disorganised attachment behaviours

Child's behaviour	Adult's behaviour
• Appears contradictory or frozen • Screams by the door for parent, then moves away on reunion • Approaches parent, then stops suddenly and 'freezes' for 15–20 seconds • Approaches parent, but holds hands up in front of face or averts head • Sinks to floor, rocking on hands and knees. • Child may be motionless/silent, does not respond when handled by the parent	• Appears disconnected or insensitive • Fails to take initiative in approaching infant • Hesitant, or tries to deflect infant's attempt at contact • Behaviour suggests fear of child – timid, deferential • Lack of response to child – frozen response, handling the child as an inanimate object • Negative intrusive behaviour – gets too close, overrides child's cues, continually takes over • Sexualised/romantic behaviours • Disorganised behaviour (e.g. contradiction between behaviour and verbal message) • Hostile, rejecting comments – parent angry, frustrated, shows disgust • Frightening/threatening behaviour, physical or verbal

Adapted from Shemmings and Shemmings (2011, pp31–49)

Some promising interventions being developed to help parents develop reflective function in interaction with their children include the VIPP (Video Intervention to Promote Positive Parenting) approach (Shemmings et al., 2012; C4EO and WAVE Trust, 2010), backed by research that shows significant improvements in sensitivity (Kalinauskiene et al., 2009; Barlow et al., 2008).

Targeted and responsive safeguarding: multi-agency working

The importance of effective multi-agency working has been consistently stressed in inquiry reports (Laming, 2003 and 2009; Munro, 2011a, 2011b) and serious case reviews (Reder et al., 1993; Ofsted, 2010), and it has been a key theme in recent policy. While being especially important for the Designated Key Person and the manager of each setting, it is important that other staff develop these skills too. Much of this will happen on a day-to-day basis, but two key multi-disciplinary meetings often form the focus of such work at the targeted level of safeguarding (CAF/TAC meetings) or the responsive level (case conferences). As the CAF process is detailed in Chapter 2 we will consider the skills for case conferences here, but they are applicable in any multi-agency meeting.

Case conferences are held following an investigation of abuse/neglect where a child could be at risk of future significant harm. They bring together parents and key professionals, of whom you could be one, to share information about the concerns and findings of any investigation. Wider information about the family is also shared, and a decision made on the level of risk and whether to make the child/children 'subject to a child protection plan'. If so, the meeting would then outline what the key steps of this plan should be, and appoint a key worker to co-ordinate its implementation and regular review.

Case conferences have many advantages, helping to share information quickly in such a way that separate pieces of knowledge held by different agencies and the family can be put together to help clarify patterns of behaviour and concern. They also involve the parents (and children where they are old enough) in the process, help to manage the anxiety experienced by both the family and professionals by using a team approach, and allow resources and support to be contributed appropriately.

But there are also disadvantages. There is a definite hierarchy, in which Children's Social Care, police and experts such as child psychologists may form a high status 'group within the group', whereas 'peripheral contact professionals', such as the school nurse or foster carer, tend to be lower status – and this can affect the value placed on their information and opinions.

ACTIVITY 4

List possible attendees at a case conference. Highlight those you think may be high status. Then highlight who knows the child best. Is there any pattern here?

Now compare your answer to the suggested one at the end of this chapter.

As an early years professional you have a unique perspective to offer, as you may be one of the few people in the room who actually know the child well. The social worker and health visitor may only see the child irregularly, and one of the key reasons for concern may be that the parent is not in touch with their child's needs. Your unique perspective is only one of several, so it's crucial to value a team approach, but you can feel confident knowing that your input is important. You may hold crucial information, based on your day-to-day knowledge of the child – on their development, any changes in behaviour and interaction with the parent. Recent research on serious case reviews (Brandon et al., 2012) highlights the lack of child development teaching on professional courses for social workers and teachers, and a lack of consistency in child development training for health visitors. So be confident about the value of your contribution. You may be best placed to act as the 'voice of the child' by putting across your view of what the child needs to the conference.

The more confidently you put forward your views, and support them with facts from your observations and underpinning knowledge, the more the conference will respect your views and ultimately this will help ensure the best outcome for the child. It is important to give a balanced view, acknowledging genuine positives in family functioning as well as difficulties and concerns. As the parent will usually accept the invitation to be present, it is important to prepare them for what you intend to say by sharing with them the written report you prepare for the conference, and meeting with them to discuss the report beforehand if this is possible and safe for you to do so. This ensures there are no surprises on the day, and helps you share information at the conference without worrying about what the parent's reaction might be. Write your report as a brief but accurate summary, avoiding (or explaining) jargon. It's perfectly acceptable to read from your report and notes when asked to contribute at the conference, as again this helps you present a clear account – speak clearly and take your time. Talk to parents normally during the meeting, using their names, rather than talking 'about' them. Listen to other people's contributions and consider what they say carefully. Ask questions if you don't understand, as it's likely that others will be uncertain too and you will be doing them a favour by voicing these questions.

But it is at the risk-assessment and decision-making end of the case conference that more complicated dynamics can be most apparent, unless the meeting is well chaired. Two dynamics are identified in the literature. One is 'groupthink' (Janis, 1982) where a desire to avoid conflict overrides a realistic appraisal of alternative views or actions – and members of the group either self-censor and do not offer alternatives, or the group disregards or discounts any contrary opinion expressed. Research on group decision-making using simple line-length matching tasks (Asch, 1955) provided evidence on how only 25 per cent of subjects were confident enough to always give the correct answer in the face of group pressure.

Interestingly, when just one other member of the group also gave the correct answer, it empowered the 'subject' to trust their judgement. So if you have a different opinion in a meeting, share it and give evidence to support what you say as this might help others to speak out too. If parents are faced with all the professionals agreeing they may resent that the decision has already been taken as a fait accompli – so an open and fair consideration of alternatives will help them.

The other dynamic is a tendency for groups to reach consensus around the first opinion confidently expressed, creating a 'bandwagon' effect, perhaps because this acts to reduce stress and uncertainty. The first opinion would usually be expressed by one of the more 'powerful' members of the group, who are usually not the ones who know the child best, so again, going against this dynamic by giving a different view may bring about a better outcome for the child. Conferences often make very careful and well-evidenced decisions but there may be very good justifications to speak up if you think the meeting is overlooking something, particularly to support the child.

Responsive safeguarding: your part in the safety plan

If a child is made 'subject to a child protection plan' as a result of a case conference then a plan will be outlined and agreed either at the end of the conference or in a separate meeting of key professionals and the family soon after. While highly dependent on the child's situation and needs, it might typically include: legal decisions and any court action, where the child will live (e.g. placement with relatives or foster carers), practical help (e.g. housing issues, safety equipment), any therapeutic help for the child (e.g. play therapy), parenting skills (such as Incredible Years), work with the parent and child together (such as Parent-Child Interaction Therapy) , and individual support/therapy for the adults or whole family (counselling, Family Nurse Partnerships). Key workers frequently use a contract approach, making it clear what is required of the family in terms of changes in the care of the child, but also what support the family can expect from professionals in order to achieve these changes. Your role in such a plan may include anything from a continued or extended offer of day-care, with clear arrangements for reporting any missed sessions, to the supervision of contact visits or the provision of parenting skills sessions if you work in a Children's Centre.

Some local authorities in England and Wales are adopting an approach from Australia called Signs of Safety (Turnell and Edwards, 1999; Turnell, 2012). This is an attempt to create detailed safety plans, agreed with families, which balance the focus between concerns and strengths. In line with future directions recommended in the Munro Report (2011b) it creates plans that can be understood by children and they, along with the wider family and family friends, may have an active role in the plan where appropriate. The plan is written in everyday language, with straightforward rules and actions, with pictures to help engage everyone involved.

Two recent UK reviews (DCSF, 2009b; Gardner, 2008) show concern that *recent emphasis on strengths-based approaches and the positive aspects of families (for example in the Common Assessment Framework) arguably discourages workers from making professional judgments about deficits in parents' behaviour which might be endangering their children* (DCSF, 2009b, p47). Both reviews suggest Signs of Safety is the one approach that incorporates a strengths-based focus balanced with an exploration of danger and risk. Ofsted inspections (e.g. in North Yorkshire) have commented on the strength of analysis that comes from the approach (Ofsted, 2011b) and Gateshead was mentioned by Munro for its improved practice as a result of the consistent use of the approach (Munro, 2011a).

Responsive safeguarding: effects of abuse/neglect

The effects of abuse, and children's reactions to it, vary widely. The child's age, level of development and resilience make a difference. Similarly factors to do with the abuse itself – its type, frequency, duration, severity and the relationship the child has to the abuser – are important. The level of support available to the child is a major variable: whether parents and other adults believed them and have given emotional support since, any therapy provided, the quality of healthcare and support in the community such as schools, early years settings and religious groups the family may be involved with. But no effects are automatic. We have considered already how we can make a difference to a child's level of resilience. After any abuse, the level of support we offer can also plays a major role in a child's recovery.

Table 8.2 in Activity 5 below lists the most common effects of abuse/neglect on young children, but note that it contains effects that might occur across the whole range of abuse and neglect – any one child will only show some of these.

ACTIVITY 5

Imagine a child in your care suffering from the effects shown in Table 8.2.
Add ideas of your own in the right-hand column on how to support them with each.

Table 8.2 Negative effects of abuse/neglect on young children

	Short-term	Long-term	How we can support children
Physical	• Minor to severe injury • Concussion • Breathing difficulties	• Permanent physical injury • Learning disabilities • Impaired brain development (especially areas involved in emotion and memory) • Poor physical health/development	
Psychological	• Fear • Lack of trust • Hyper-vigilant • Loss • Regression • Self-blame	• Stress/anger issues • Hyper-arousal • Sleep disturbance • Anxiety/panic disorders • Post-Traumatic Stress Disorder • Withdrawn • Over-compliant • Compulsive behaviour • Lack of concentration • Delayed emotional/language/development • Low self-esteem • Depression • Attachment difficulties	

Now compare your answer to the suggested one at the end of this chapter.

Your own ideas, and those given in the comparison answer can help gradually heal the effects in most children, especially alongside any specific help they may receive (see 'Other Professional Support' later). However, if you have tried your best and the child is not progressing, then it is in their interests for you to refer them for specialist help.

In whatever setting you work it is also important to communicate closely with the parent/carer. A joint discussion involving parents and the social worker at the outset can make setting policies and your professional role in any protection plan clear, so that contacting Children's Social Care if the child does not attend is discussed and understood. Thereafter make parents feel welcome and be non-judgemental. This is not so easy in practice, but thoughts that might help are: they may have unresolved trauma from their own childhoods; the non-abusing parent may genuinely not have known; and, ultimately, your only effective way to improve the child's care where the child is to remain at home is by supporting change in the parents' behaviour, so you do what is necessary to achieve that. The key person plays a crucial role in being available to listen if parents want to talk and ask questions. Equally, sharing information back to parents about the child's reactions while in your care and what actions you are taking and why, keeps the parent fully informed and encourages a consistent approach. If you work in a children's centre then supporting them directly with parenting tasks, demonstrating skills clearly and giving genuine praise for changes is crucial.

ACTIVITY 6

Using the action plan template from previous chapters enter any further actions you might want to take to learn more about or practise some of the issues/skills that have been covered in the previous sections.

Responsive safeguarding: other professional support

The key elements of any support for a child and their family after abuse will be outlined in the Child Protection Plan and any more detailed safety plan that might be developed. While much of this will involve monitoring and support from social workers, health professionals, schools and Children's Centre staff, some specialist services may also be required. However, the reality is that therapeutic services are underfunded, with a shortfall of therapeutic provision for sexual abuse alone estimated at between 51,715 and 88,544 places (Allnock et al., 2009), with particular shortages in some areas of the country and for some groups of children (those from ethnic minorities or with special needs). For therapeutic work with parents, or for whole families, the picture is similar.

However, where therapeutic services do exist they can be very valuable. To help children express their feelings, and challenge negative thought patterns as a result of abuse there is considerable evidence to support the effectiveness of cognitive behaviour therapy (CBT) approaches, particularly for sexual abuse (MacMillan et al., 2009; MacMillan, 2010) and it is the treatment of choice listed by the National Institute for Clinical Excellence (2005). Intensive foster-care approaches such as Multi-Dimensional Treatment Foster-Care (Allen, 2011a; Fisher et al., 2005) show improved outcomes, as does play therapy, particularly where it actively involves the parent (Bratton et al., 2005), but less so for physical abuse.

For families and parents the Family Nurse Partnership home visiting programme, which supports first-time mothers from before birth to two years, has been shown to prevent maltreatment (MacMillan et al., 2009; Allen, 2011a). There is also good evidence for the Incredible Years and Triple P – Positive Parenting Programmes, various schools of Family Therapy, and Parent Child Interaction Therapy (MacMillan et al., 2009; MacMillan, 2010; Allen, 2011a).

Effective interventions to prevent the reoccurrence of emotional abuse and neglect are still quite limited (MacMillan, 2010) although some approaches used to support families variously labelled as 'multi-problem' or 'chaotic' may prove useful, such as Family Intervention Projects (NatCen, 2010) and the Life Project in Swindon (Life, 2012; Bunting, 2011).

Context: current and future policy directions

We began this chapter by considering how safeguarding policy developed up to 2010, noting some grounds for optimism. We currently have different political directions set by the Coalition government in the context of spending cuts whose effects are only just beginning to impact. What future direction is safeguarding likely to take, and how does this effect young children and the professionals working with them?

An early internal memo within the DfE detailed changes in the language to be used to refer to children's issues under the Coalition government. These included the phrase 'safeguarding' being changed back to 'child protection' (Puffett, 2010). While this may seem minor, language can be significant in determining future directions. Any move from 'safeguarding' to 'child protection' would suggest a narrower focus on 'risk' and 'significant harm', and a decrease in the priority of early intervention/preventative approaches. What evidence exists by which to judge if this is the direction being taken?

No one set of professionals can realistically be tasked with ensuring children's safety, and the principle of safeguarding being 'everyone's business' has been one of the key influences leading to better outcomes. A strong concern raised in responses to the government's consultation on the revised 'Working Together to Safeguard Children' guidance (DfE, 2012) is that the tone of the document seems to move away from a 'whole system' approach to one where social workers and local authorities are responsible, albeit with support from other agencies (LGA, 2012). Other sector responses put this more starkly: *It is about dismantling a system of shared responsibility for children's safety and replacing it with an ill-defined free-for-all* (Ennals, 2012).

Other current initiatives may create additional barriers to effective multi-agency working, including the restructuring of the NHS. Care services increasingly being delivered by voluntary groups and private providers and the growth in academy and free schools – some of whom will not have taken any role in safeguarding processes before – add to this trend. During this transition strong national guidance that stresses shared responsibility may be particularly important. Any gaps in national guidance are likely to lead to local councils, sectors and settings filling the 'void' by developing their own guidance, with the risk of inconsistency (LGA, 2012).

With regard to early intervention the Allen Review (2011a, 2011b), commissioned by the Coalition government, shows some commitment to prevention. The government's response to the review was set out within the 'Supporting Families in the Foundation Years' document (DfE, 2011a, 2011c). Key actions, and their progress, are summarised in Table 8.3.

Table 8.3 Supporting Families in the Foundation Years

Target	Progress
Reduced early intervention grant funding	11% cut overall in Early Intervention Grant for 2011–12, but not 'ring-fenced' and since reduced further to fund free places for disadvantaged two year olds. Local authorities can use it to protect other services, but some may use it creatively for early intervention
Increase in health visitors by 4,200 posts from 8,092 (May 2010) to 12,292 (by April 2015)	Minimal increase to 8,199 (March 2012) (DoH, 2012a), but 1,642 currently on training programmes in 2011/12
Double number of families receiving Family Nurse Partnership (from 6,500 to 13,000) by 2015	Currently 9,000 families receiving FNP service (DoH, 2012b), but Allen Report suggests 30,000 families could benefit (Allen, 2011)
Extend 15 hours free early education to all disadvantaged two year olds (130,000 by September 2013 and 260,000 by 2014–15)	Providers have concerns whether level of funding for the places will cover the costs, so will fill current capacity but less likely to invest in extra places – DfE officials estimate 40,000 shortfall in places for September 2013
Retain network of Sure Start Children's Centres, but with new core purpose of early intervention and outreach	Centre numbers reduced from 3,631 in April 2010 to 3,507 in September 2011 (DfE, 2011b); many local authorities now have one manager for several sites, and centres may not be open a full week More recent estimates suggest more than 400 may be closed (Butler, 2013)

In conclusion, against the background of government cutbacks, the continued funding here still shows some commitment to early intervention, although there is already evidence to suggest that many Children's Centres are now saving money by delivering programmes they have devised or adapted themselves, using untrained staff or volunteers, rather than evidence-based programmes (Jackson, 2012).

However, this needs to be set against the background of welfare benefit cuts which includes caps on housing benefit, a benefit cap irrespective of family size and the introduction of Universal Credit. The Institute for Fiscal Studies, a body with a reputation for independence, predicts increases in child poverty of between 400,000 and 500,000 (depending on measure used) between 2010/11 and 2015/16 (Browne, 2012), and even the government's own staff estimate an extra 100,000 children in poverty as a result of the benefit cap alone (Boffey and McVeigh, 2012). Save the Children, whose work usually supports children on health and hunger issues across the world, has for the first time launched a campaign for children in poverty in the UK (Save the Children, 2012). Eileen Munro, who undertook the review of child protection on behalf of the government, has expressed concern that these pressures on families will lead to greater numbers of child abuse referrals (Higgs, 2012).

Munro's own key proposals for change are mainly ones that will affect Children's Social Care, with more emphasis on the quality of assessments of families and more flexibility with procedures and timescales to allow this to be achieved. She stresses the importance of forming meaningful relationships with families and particularly with children, so they are informed and their views taken into account and represented in planning and decision-making meetings.

Probably the most relevant theme here for early years staff is the greater emphasis on listening to children, and there has been much discussion of children's rights approaches being at the heart of all safeguarding practice, particularly Article 12 of the UNCRC – the right to express their views freely. For early years staff it is important that day-to-day practice upholds children's rights, and our skills of listening to children both verbally and through their body language and play can also prove valuable when presenting the 'child's voice' at multi-agency meetings.

ACTIVITY 7

The UNCRC Article 27 gives children the right to a standard of living adequate for the child's physical, mental, spiritual, moral and social development. Do you think the current government upholds this? Have previous governments done so?

The UNCRC does allow governments to achieve article 27, 'in accordance with national conditions and within their means', so governments vary in the priority given to children's well-being and living standards. In terms of current policy directions there are very real concerns, partly about funding cuts, but more seriously around the predicted growth in child poverty. But there are also grounds for optimism, with local authorities prepared to be creative with their greater professional and budgetary flexibility.

A recent example here is that of Kirklees in West Yorkshire who are to extend the offer of free childcare for children up to the age of 14 (18 for those with SEND) whose parents are on Jobseeker's Allowance. This allows them to take up training, volunteering and interviews without the worry about childcare costs. The extended age-limit has been possible due to the ability to use the early intervention monies more flexibly (Mahadevan, 2012).

There is evidence (Munro, 2012) of several local authorities developing more co-operative working practices and teamwork approaches to encourage greater reflection on improving practice, along the lines of the Reclaiming Social Work approach (Goodman and Trowler, 2012). Similarly 12 local authorities are implementing the Signs of Safety approach in 2012, with others planning to follow (Munro, 2012).

CHAPTER SUMMARY

In this chapter we have explored the policy context with regard to safeguarding and shown its links to our own daily practice within the sector. We have considered some areas of theory and research (e.g. disorganised attachment and 'what works'), new approaches (e.g. safety planning) and how best to work with children to encourage resilience or recovery. This can inform and strengthen our contributions when working with other agencies, which can only gain the early years sector greater respect, helping to ensure safe practice and improved outcomes for young children.

Self-assessment questions

1. What practical steps can be taken to maximise the safeguarding of all children in an early years setting?
2. What four processes stop professionals either recognising situations of harm or taking action about them – and what can be done to counteract these?
3. List three ways that 'disorganised attachment' may be indicated in children's behaviour, and three ways it may be identified in adults' behaviour.

FURTHER READING

Jozwiak, G (2012) Two-year-old entitlement to be funded by cut to Early Intervention Grant, *Children and Young People Now*. Available at: **www.cypnow.co.uk/cyp/news/1074769/two-entitlement-funded-cut-intervention-grant** (accessed 3 January 2013).

Mortimer, J, North, M, Katz, A and Stead, J (2012) *You Have Someone to Trust: Outstanding Safeguarding Practice in Primary Schools*. London: Office of the Children's Commissioner – report on a study of best practice in safeguarding in primary schools.

Office of the Children's Commissioner (2012) *Practical Tips for Schools from the Report: You Have Someone to Trust – Outstanding Safeguarding Practice in Primary Schools*. London: Office of the Children's Commissioner – companion report to that listed above.

Rushforth, C (2012) *Safeguarding and Child Protection in the Early Years*. London: Practical Pre-School Books – excellent sections on new staff induction, effective leadership and management for safeguarding, and supervision.

Wilson, K (ed.) (2007) *The Child Protection Handbook*, 3rd edn. Oxford: Ballière Tindall – thorough and detailed.

Activity answers

Activity 3: Information Sharing (DCSF, 2008d, sec 3.36) states consent need not be sought if this would: place a person (child, family member, yourself, a third party) at increased risk of harm / significant harm; prejudice the prevention, detection or prosecution of a serious crime; or lead to an unjustified delay in making enquiries about allegations of significant harm to a child. If consent is asked and refused you may still lawfully share information 'in the public interest' – including to protect a child from significant harm (sec 3.38-3.39). Ultimately you will not be criticised professionally for having given the child the benefit of the doubt even if concerns later prove to be unsubstantiated.

Activity 4: Possible attendees at a Case Conference might be: Chair, Social Worker/ Senior, Police, Doctor, Child Psychologist, Health Visitor, Local Authority Solicitor, Probation Officer, *Teachers, Early Years Worker, Foster Carer, Parents* & Supporter, Minute Taker.

These are roughly in 'hierarchy order'. The ones who usually know the child best are given in italics – but are less likely to have influence over decisions.

Activity 5:

	Short-term	Long-term	How we can support children
Physical	• Minor to severe injury • Concussion • Breathing difficulties	• Permanent physical injury • Learning disabilities • Impaired brain development (especially areas involved in emotion and memory) • Poor physical health/ development	• Physical care/medication required for any injury • Regular meals/snacks • Encourage exercise within limits of any injuries/conditions
Psychological	• Fear • Lack of trust • Hyper-vigilant • Loss • Regression • Self-blame	• Stress/anger issues • Hyper-arousal • Sleep disturbance • Anxiety/panic disorders • Post-Traumatic Stress Disorder • Withdrawn • Over-compliant • Compulsive behaviour • Lack of concentration • Delayed emotional/ language/intellectual development • Low self-esteem • Depression • Attachment difficulties	• Don't single child out/draw attention, but do observe – e.g. for patterns/ triggers that make them angry or anxious • Give verbal reassurance, make sure any physical comfort is child's choice ('would you like...?') • Try to enable happy, ordinary times • Consistent routines, especially at first so they predict what will happen and feel in control, consult about any changes • Consistent team approach to behaviour, with clear rules • Cat nap space/chill-out area • Raise self-esteem – give genuine praise, choose tasks and responsibilities they can succeed with, requiring only a short attention span initially

	Short-term	Long-term	How we can support children
Psychological			• Listen to child – talk about feelings, e.g. in circle time, so they understand feelings are okay • If they talk about abuse, listen and reassure them it wasn't their fault • Allow safe expression of feelings – persona dolls and puppets (including scary characters to help them play out their fears), music/dancing, painting, play-doh, outdoor play, rough play using soft-play equipment • Give choices where possible, so child has sense of control • Don't make an issue of any regressive or compulsive behaviour (wetting, hand-washing) • Plan for gradual catch-up in social skills/developmental delays • Encourage shared activities gradually if child is withdrawn

9 The aspiring leader: taking your practice further

Rose Envy

Reading through this chapter will help you to:

- critically reflect upon the definition of leadership and management within the context of early years;
- critically reflect upon the skills and knowledge required to become effective early years practitioners in line with the EYP standards.

Introduction: defining leadership

The purpose of this discussion is not to agree a definitive definition of leadership; rather, it is to make a distinction between leadership and management and explore the differences between the two concepts, relating these to early years practice.

ACTIVITY 1

Reflect upon the terms leadership and management. What is your understanding of them? Write down a few words which you associate with each term.

Firstly, let us explore the notion of 'management'. Coleman (2005) suggests that management focus upon the operational issues of an organisation, that is the structures, policies, procedures, finance and resources within an organisation. Within an early years setting in the private sector, these tasks would usually be the responsibility of the nursery manager, within a school context it would be the head teacher and within a Children's Centre, the operational tasks would be the responsibility of the centre manager. Leadership is often the subject of much debate as it is not so easy to associate leadership with specific tasks. The notion of leadership is much more abstract and has often been linked to the creation of an organisational culture (Coleman, 2005) or, as Thomas (2001) suggests, it is about using our personal power to win the hearts and minds of people to achieve a common purpose. In early years we use our personal power to motivate staff and children to generate feelings of excitement, challenge, ownership, commitment and involvement. We do this by giving them a clear understanding of what they have to do and why it is important to do it. We also have to motivate some parents to encourage them to take an active role in their child's learning both within the setting and at home.

If management is concerned with tasks associated with the operational aspects of early years practice and leadership is concerned with creating an environment where practitioners are motivated and inspired to work cooperatively to ensure that children receive the best possible care and education they deserve, can early years settings operate efficiently and effectively when either management or leadership is absent?

ACTIVITY 2

Begin to consider early years practice. Think about an early years setting with:

(a) good management but little or no leadership;
(b) poor management but strong leadership.

For each scenario consider how the staff would feel, what Ofsted inspectors might report and what might parents notice.

In an early years setting where there is good management, financial systems and procedures would be in place, the setting would have a clear business plan, all policies would be reviewed and updated annually, and the practitioners would know exactly what to do and when to do it. However, there would be no long-term vision for the setting, that is how it would remain sustainable or how practitioners would seek to continually improve the quality of care and education they provide. Practitioners may feel demotivated as there may be no long-term view of how their professional development would progress and there may not be opportunities for progression within the organisation. Where there was good leadership and poor management, practitioners would have a clear vision for the future of the setting but there would be little or no concern as to how the vision would be realised. The setting may be under-resourced and parents would perceive the setting to be disorganised.

CASE STUDY 1

Little Gems Nursery was a company limited by guarantee and was located on the site of a primary school. The head teacher of the school approached the Childcare Strategy Manager within the local authority expressing concern that she had received complaints from parents regarding letters they had received from the nursery requesting the payment of nursery fees for their child. The parents claimed that they had already paid their fees.

At the end of each week the nursery manager would the check the fees paid against the number of children attending nursery for that week. It was during this process that the nursery manager discovered that there was a deficit in the amount of fees collected compared with the number of children attending the setting. To try and identify which parents had not paid their child's nursery fees, all those parents who paid by cash were sent letters from the manager requesting payment of fees. This caused great concern among the parents.

The Business Support Advisor was asked to visit the setting. To his dismay, it became apparent that the nursery manager did not have adequate systems in place to record fees

---

CASE STUDY 1 *continued*

paid and did not give parents receipts upon payment of fees. This was cause for concern because those parents who paid by cash had no way to prove that they had paid their fees.

Little Gems Nursery did not have clear management systems in place to record and administer the nursery fees.

CASE STUDY 2

Extract from an Ofsted Report 2008

The leadership and management of the early years provision

The required policies and procedures are in place. Staff have a very clear knowledge of these, especially in relation to safeguarding children from harm. Suitable recruitment, vetting and induction procedures are in place and the ongoing suitability of staff is appropriately monitored. In general, safety is very good. Staff show a clear understanding of related policies and procedures, such as the collection of children and a lost child. Security is very good, for example an electronic lock secures the entrance into the nursery and only staff have the entry code. Staff are vigilant and they ensure that students are supervised closely and that visitors are screened and do not have unsupervised contact with children. Staff qualification requirements and ratios are very well maintained. Staff are effectively deployed and work efficiently together as a team. They benefit from annual appraisals, regular supervision sessions, frequent team meetings and an open and supportive leadership style. Staff have access to relevant training opportunities and they are keen to continue to develop their knowledge and very good practice. Records are up-to-date and very well organised. Effective methods for the assessment of the provision are in place and involve the provider, management, staff and parents. Strengths and areas for development are clearly identified and action plans collated. The setting shows a real commitment to the continuous improvement of the service, care and education provided.

Ofsted (2008)

From the discussion and case studies above, it is clear that leadership and management are two distinct and complementary functions within early years settings. For settings to remain sustainable, continually improve the quality of care and education they provide, and encourage staff retention, it is essential that there is strong leadership and management with the setting.

In Chapter 1 we made reference to EYPS, stating that, if as an early years practitioner you wish to take your practice further to become a graduate practitioner with EYPS, you needed to demonstrate that you are competent in all areas of practice as identified within the EYPS Standards. In relation to leadership and management, to achieve EYPS you will need to demonstrate that you are able to:

8   *Lead practice and foster a culture of continuous improvement.*

8.1   *Model and implement effective practice, and support and mentor other practitioners.*

8.2   *Reflect on the effectiveness of provision, propose appropriate changes and influence, shape and support the implementation of policies and practices within the setting.*

8.3   *Take responsibility for improving practice through appropriate professional development, for self and colleagues.*

8.4   *Promote equality of opportunity through championing children's rights and anti-discriminatory practice.*

8.5   *Understand the implications of relevant legislation, statutory frameworks, including the EYFS, and policy for early years settings and apply in practice.*

DfE (2012d, p4)

Leadership within early years settings

ACTIVITY 3

Begin to consider early years practice. How might leadership be the responsibility of more than one person?

Within early years settings, leadership is often the responsibility of more than one person, that is leadership is shared across the team. For example, practitioners are often employed as room leaders or room supervisors and are responsible for leading the practice and staff within a particular room, that is in the baby room or pre-school room. Practitioners who have a particular interest in a specific area of the Early Years Foundation Stage framework may be given responsibility for leading the pedagogy (teaching and learning) in that area, for example outdoor play. Additionally, the setting will have a graduate practitioner who has achieved EYPS who will take responsibility for leading pedagogy across all age ranges. All practitioners who have a leadership role will not work in isolation from each other or from other staff but will work collaboratively, interacting on a daily basis to ensure that children receive high-quality play and learning experiences. Delegating areas of leadership responsibility to several practitioners within the setting underpins the concept of 'distributed leadership' (Spillane, 2005).

THEORY FOCUS

Distributed leadership

Distributed leadership is often associated with the terms 'shared leadership' or 'team leadership'. The example above demonstrates how various leadership responsibilities can

---

THEORY FOCUS *continued*

be shared across the early years team. However, Spillane (2005) argues that distributed leadership is not so much concerned with the various roles and responsibilities which are assigned to individuals within a team. Rather it is concerned with leadership practice, that is how those with leadership responsibilities interact with each other and with the staff they lead. We have also suggested above that early years leaders will not work in isolation from each other or from other staff. This view is further supported by Spillane who states that:

> *leadership takes the form of the interactions between leaders and followers, rather than as a function of one or more leaders.*

(Spillane, 2005, p147)

The underpinning assumptions within distributed leadership acknowledge that leadership is not merely the responsibility of one person but advocates that leadership occurs across an organisation as identified above.

To further explore the notion of distributed leadership, follow this link to Spillane et al. (2001) at: **http://edr.sagepub.com/content/30/3/23**.

Everyone a leader: leading learning

We have previously discussed how leadership can be shared between practitioners within early years settings, identifying the different roles and responsibilities which can be delegated to staff. The focus of this discussion will be to explore the notion that all practitioners within early years settings are leaders, irrespective of their job role and the level of responsibility they hold.

ACTIVITY 4

Begin to consider early years practice. Think of an example when you adopted the role of leader. Who and what were you leading and how did you do this?

All early years practitioners are leaders of learning, that is all practitioners lead and support children's learning and development. We do this by following the child's interests and by being involved in meaningful interactions which will develop children's thinking and enable them to solve problems or develop their ideas further. Siraj-Blatchford et al. (2002) suggest that both children and practitioners must work together collaboratively and be equally involved in interactions. The process of Sustained Shared Thinking (SST) requires that practitioners are not only aware of the child's interests, but that they must be able to follow those interests if they are to help children develop their ideas or solve a problem.

ACTIVITY 5

Follow the link below and watch the short video clip of sustained shared thinking in action. What do you notice about the practitioners?

www.youtube.com/watch?v=SmZsDfVTa8I

In the video you will notice how the practitioner becomes completely involved in the child's activity, following instructions and asking pertinent questions which encourage the child to extend the activity further. The principles of SST can be linked to the underpinning principles of Vygotsky's theory of cognitive development as discussed in Chapter 3, specifically in relation to the concepts of a 'More Knowledgeable Other' and the Zone of Proximal Development. Effective SST requires that the practitioner completely immerses him or herself in the child's activity and to do this you will need to overcome any embarrassment you may feel. Also, to be involved in effective SST, you must ask open-ended questions which encourage the child to expand upon their ideas, therefore good communication skills are essential when leading learning.

Good communication skills help leaders of learning to create a culture which:

- fosters good relationships with children;
- ensures that children are actively engaged in conversation;
- ensures that the opinions, ideas and views of children are respected and valued.

To achieve EYPS, practitioners we required to be confident and competent in engaging SST with children.

Standard 4 states that practitioners must:

4. *Set high expectations which inspire, motivate and challenge every child.*
4.1 *Establish and sustain a stimulating and inclusive environment where children feel confident and are able to learn and develop.*
4.2 *Engage in sustained shared thinking with children.*
4.3 *Give constructive feedback to help children evaluate their achievements and facilitate further learning.*
4.4 *Demonstrate the positive values, attitudes and behaviours expected from children.*

DfE (2012d, p3)

In addition to having good communication skills, Ofsted (2007, p18) recommends that leaders of learning have a sound knowledge and understanding of the EYFS, and that they recognise the strengths and weaknesses of staff. If practitioners are to be effective leaders of learning they must also recognise the strengths and areas for development of individual children and use this knowledge to identify areas of learning and development which need to be developed further. Ofsted (2007) further suggests that to effectively lead children's learning practitioners must have an awareness of the different learning styles adopted by children as discussed in Chapter 5.

Moyles et al. (2002) explain that effective leadership of learning involves everything that a practitioner does within the teaching and learning context.

Begin to consider early years practice. What tasks do you think must be done to ensure that practitioners are effective leaders of learning?

Effective leadership of learning involves the following tasks. With each task, where appropriate, reference is made to the competency statements within the EYPS standards.

Planning:

- You should provide play and learning opportunities within the learning environment which support children's learning and development. Planning should be carried out on a weekly, termly and yearly basis and involve all practitioners and children. Planning should be flexible to enable the children's interests to be taken into consideration and relate to both the indoor and outdoor learning environment.

EYPS Standard 6 states that practitioners must:

6. *Plan provision taking account of the individual needs of every child*
6.1 *Provide balanced and flexible daily and weekly routines that meet children's needs and interests and enable them to learn and develop.*
6.2 *Plan and provide appropriate adult-led and child-initiated play and experiences that enable children to learn and develop.*
6.3 *Select, prepare and use a range of resources suitable for children's ages, interests and abilities, which value diversity and promote equality and inclusion.*

(DfE, 2012d, p3)

Evaluation:

- Play and learning opportunities should be evaluated to establish how effective they are in meeting children's needs. Consideration should be given to ways in which the activities can be extended, adapted to meet the needs of all children or improved.

Observation and assessment:

- You should continually observe children's play and learning to assess progress towards the learning outcomes within the EYFS. Information from observations and assessments is used to inform the learning and development opportunities to be provided which will enable children to progress.

EYPS Standard 5 states that practitioners must:

5. *Make use of observation and assessment to meet the individual needs of every child.*

5.1 *Observe, assess, record and report on progress in children's development and learning, using this to plan next steps.*

5.2 *Engage effectively with parents/carers and wider professionals in the ongoing assessment and appropriate provision for each child.*

5.3 *Differentiate provision to meet the individual needs of the child and provide opportunities to extend their learning and development.*

(DfE, 2012d, p2)

Communicating with children and their parents:

- You should take time to listen to children, proactively seek their views and find out what their interests are. Every effort should be made to try to incorporate children's interests into session plans.
- You should also encourage parents to be involved in their children's learning, so that they are equipped to support their children's learning at home.

EYPS Standard 2 states that practitioners should:

2. *Work directly with children and in partnership with their families to facilitate learning and support development.*

2.1 *Understand the important influence of parents/carers, engaging them effectively to support their child's well-being, learning and development.*

2.2 *Communicate effectively with children from birth to age five, listening and responding sensitively.*

2.3 *Promote positive social and emotional behaviour, attitudes and independence.*

2.4 *Know and understand the significance of attachment and how effectively to promote it.*

2.5 *Develop and sustain respectful relationships with children and their families.*

(DfE, 2012d, p1)

All early years practitioners should be able to lead and support children's learning and development whether they aspire to achieve EYPS or not. In addition to the skills and knowledge identified above, all leaders of learning, particularly those wishing to achieve EYPS, must be able to demonstrate that they meet EYPS Standard 1, that is:

1. *Support the healthy growth and development of children from birth to the age of five.*

1.1 *Know and understand how children learn and develop and how this can be affected by individual circumstances.*

1.2 *Support individual children through all areas of learning and development as outlined in the EYFS.*

1.3 *Encourage and support children's learning in ways that are appropriate to their development.*

1.4 *Support children through a range of transitions.*

1.5 *Know when a child is in need of support and when to refer to other relevant services.*

(DfE, 2012d, p1)

The role of a practitioner who has achieved EYPS is very diverse and somewhat different to that of a qualified teacher. If as an early years practitioner you feel that you would like to progress your career further but would rather concentrate on teaching and learning, as a graduate with a good degree, that is a classification of 2:1 or above, you can apply to study towards Qualified Teacher Status (QTS). Just as an EYP must demonstrate that they are competent in meeting EYPS standards, as a trainee teacher you will be required to demonstrate that you meet the required standards as defined by the Department for Education (2012c). There are some similarities between EYPS Standards and Teachers' Standards; some examples are presented in Table 9.1.

Table 9.1 Teachers' Standards 1 and EYPS Standard 4

Teachers' Standard 1	EYPS Standard 4
1. Have high expectations which inspire, motivate and challenge pupils	4. Set high expectations which inspire, motivate and challenge every child.
• establish a safe and stimulating environment for pupils, rooted in mutual respect	4.1 Establish and sustain a stimulating and inclusive environment where children feel confident and are able to learn and develop.
• set goals that stretch and challenge pupils of all backgrounds, abilities and dispositions	4.2 Engage in sustained shared thinking with children.
• demonstrate consistently the positive attitudes, values and behaviour which are expected of pupils	4.3 Give constructive feedback to help children evaluate their achievements and facilitate further learning.
	4.4 Demonstrate the positive values, attitudes and behaviours expected from children.

Adapted from DfE (2012c, p7) and DfE (2012d, p2)

Leading learning: how do leadership styles influence learning?

In the previous section we discussed some of the skills required to lead learning. We also identified some of the standards required to achieve EYPS and QTS. Lewin (1939) suggested that effective teaching and learning is not only dependent upon the practitioner's skills, but to an extent also depends upon the atmosphere which the practitioner creates to promote learning.

ACTIVITY 7

Begin to consider early years practice. EYPS Standard 4 and Teachers' Standard 1 require that the practitioner create an ethos which inspires and motivates children. How might you as a leader of learning inspire and motivate children?

Lewin (1939) identified three distinct leadership styles: autocratic, democratic and laissez-faire. In this next discussion we will outline the characteristics associated with each of these styles in relation to leading learning. Firstly, autocratic or authoritative leaders identify what tasks or activities the children will carry out; they will also dictate how they are to be done. They will make all decisions regarding planning without involving practitioners or children. In contrast, democratic leaders of learning will offer guidance to both the children and practitioners and involve them in the planning process. They will also allow children and practitioners the freedom to carry out tasks rather than dictating how they are to be done. Finally, laissez-faire leaders involve all children and all practitioners in the planning process; however, they will not take responsibility for making a final decision. In addition, the laissez-faire leader will not define the roles and responsibilities for each practitioner.

ACTIVITY 8

Begin to consider early years practice. Think about the characteristics associated with each leadership style. How might your style of leadership impact on children's learning?

Kurt Lewin's study 'Experiments in Social Space' (Lewin, 1939) highlighted the impact that each leadership style has upon children's learning. Lewin suggested that an autocratic leader stifles children's learning insofar as children are not given the opportunity to think for themselves, that is the autocratic leader dictates what activities will be done and how these will be carried out . This style of leadership does not foster an ethos which inspires or motivates children. Rather the impact that this style has upon children is demotivating because children do not feel that their interests are being taken into consideration. Also, given that an autocratic leader dictates how the activities are to be carried out, children are not encouraged to be creative because activities are always adult-led rather being both adult-led and child-initiated. This leadership style does not support the implementation of the EYFS which acknowledges that children learn and develop well in environments which respond to their individual needs and interests (DfE, 2012b). With regard to the democratic leadership style, Lewin (1939) argues that democratic leadership fosters an ethos of mutual respect between children and practitioners. Children's interests are taken into consideration during the planning process, they are allowed to be creative when carrying out tasks. Practitioners offer support and guidance to children rather than dictating what they should do and how they should carry out the activities. Leaders of learning who adopt a democratic style of leadership support the effective implementation of the EYFS which states:

> *Children learn by leading their own play, and by taking part in play which is guided by adults.*

(DfE, 2012b, p6)

ACTIVITY 9

Begin to consider early years practice. Think about the characteristics associated with laissez-faire leadership. How do you think this style of leadership will impact upon children's learning?

Within the EYFS it is stated that:

> *Each area of learning and development must be implemented through planned purposive play and through a mix of adult-led and child-initiated activities.*

(DfE, 2012b, p7)

Under laissez-faire leadership all children would be involved in the planning process which is good. However, the laissez-faire leader will not take ownership of the planning therefore there is a risk that planning will be inconsistent. There is also a risk that play will not be purposive as is required within the EYFS, that is all activities will be child-initiated and perhaps not supported by a practitioner, and as a result children's learning may not be progressed or activities may not be extended. Laissez-faire leaders do not assign roles and responsibilities to individual practitioners but it is stated within the EYFS that every child should be allocated a 'key worker' (DfE, 2012b, p7). Therefore adopting a laissez-faire style of leadership does not fulfil the requirements of the EYFS.

To help you to develop your critical thinking skills, Table 9.2 identifies some of the strengths and weaknesses associated with each leadership style.

Table 9.2 Leadership styles: strengths and weaknesses

Leadership style	Strengths	Weaknesses
Autocratic	Clear division of responsibilities Provides clear expectations of the task and how to carry it out Independent decision-making – do not take into account the views of the team	Practitioners and children do not have ownership of their work Practitioners and children lack motivation Practitioners do not feel part of the organisation
Democratic	Team members feel valued and included Team is motivated to take ownership of work Sense of belonging	Risk of not pleasing every child or practitioner
Laissez-faire	Practitioners and children could take ownership of tasks	No clear direction or vision Children and practitioners are not clear about tasks to be carried out Disorganised Indecisive

---

ACTIVITY 10

Begin to consider early years practice. Reflect upon the strengths and weaknesses associated with each leadership style. Which leadership style do you think best supports early years practice?

To foster an atmosphere of mutual respect in which children can progress their learning and development in a way that is meaningful to them, early years practitioners should adopt a democratic style of leadership. This style of leadership also promotes collaboration and co-operation between parents and practitioners and encourages parents to become involved in their children's learning. However, there may be occasions when it is both necessary and relevant for practitioners to adopt a more autocratic style of leadership; for example, if as an early years practitioner you have concerns about a child's safety or well-being you must as stated within the EYFS *notify agencies with statutory responsibilities without delay* (DfE, 2012b, p14). In addition, early years practitioners must *inform OfSTED of any allegations of serious harm or abuse by any person living, working, or looking after children on the premises* (ibid.). Ensuring safe practice is discussed in Chapter 8.

The aspiring leader: taking your practice further

Once you have achieved your early childhood studies degree, EYPS and teaching are not the only careers which you can embark upon. In Chapter 1 we identified a range of roles within Children's Services which you could aspire to, many of which include a leadership role. Whether that is leading and supporting people, practice or parents, the opportunities available to early years graduates are endless.

CASE STUDY 3

After completing her level 3 diploma in early years and childcare Claire gained employment as a nursery officer in a day nursery. Once she had gained some experience she decided to complete the Sector Endorsed Foundation Degree in Early Years Education and Care (FDAEYEC). During her studies Claire was promoted to deputy manager and as part of this role she had to deliver training to other practitioners. Claire realised that she enjoyed this part of her role, and after completing her FDAEYEC, she decided to study towards the BA (Hons) Children and Early Childhood top-up degree. During this time Claire continued to deliver training to other practitioners within the nursery. She also undertook the role of mentor to practitioners embarking upon their foundation degree.

Claire soon realised that she enjoyed her training and mentoring role more than working directly with the children so she applied for the position of early years development officer with the local authority (LA).

I have been working with the LA for 18 months and I thoroughly enjoy visiting different settings, delivering training, offering support and guidance to practitioners and sharing good practice. I really feel that I am making a difference to the lives of children by helping to improve the quality of education and care they receive.

CASE STUDY 4

After completing her Early Childhood Studies degree Lynne gained employment in the health service as a nursery nurse working with children on the paediatric ward. Lynne worked alongside play staff providing physical and emotional care to children. She also co-ordinated play activities for the children and supported parents through what is a very stressful time.

After gaining some experience as nursery nurse, Lynne decided that she would like to further her career and become a hospital play specialist. To this end, Lynne returned to part-time study and successfully achieved the Foundation Degree in Healthcare Play Specialism.

Because of her previous experience as a nursery nurse on the paediatric ward, Lynne was soon promoted to senior play specialist with the additional responsibility of leading a team of play specialists.

Lynne recalls:

> *I realised that the foundation degree was a lower level qualification than my ECS degree but I couldn't progress my career without this specialist qualification. Gaining this qualification enabled me to become registered with the Hospital Play Staff Education Trust which gives professional recognition to healthcare play staff.*

CASE STUDY 5

Antony was employed as a higher level teaching assistant (HLTA) in a local primary school. He had responsibility for leading a team of support staff and covering lessons during teacher planning, preparation and assessment (PPA) time. Antony really enjoyed this element of his work and realised that he would like to study toward achieving QTS. Antony had achieved a 2:1 classification in his ECS degree; in addition he had GCSE English, Maths and Science at grades A–C. Antony did not want to return to full-time study which was university based. Instead he wanted to complete his teacher training in school, so he applied for a place on the School-Centred Initial Teacher Training (SCITT) programme. The programme enabled Antony to spend more time training in the class-room where he could put theory into practice and build on his experiences as a HLTA.

Antony recalls:

> *While on the programme most of my teaching practice was gained in one primary school, although to broaden my experience I undertook some teaching practice in other schools which were in our school cluster. I was taught by experienced teachers which meant that my training was current.*

It is evident from the case studies above, that in order to take your practice further you must be prepared to engage in continuous professional development, whether this takes the form of studying towards formal higher-level qualifications or participating in informal training workshops to improve your knowledge and skills. As we have stated previously, the early years is a dynamic and ever-changing landscape, and to do justice to the children we work with we must ensure that at the very least we keep abreast of political and curriculum changes that impact upon our practice. Continuous professional development will not only ensure that your practice is current, it will also provide an opportunity for you to change the focus of your career as was demonstrated in each case study identified above.

The last ten years have seen unprecedented financial investment in the children's workforce. This is to ensure that the government's vision to have a *world-class children's workforce* is realised. Edmond and Price (2007) acknowledge that the term 'professional' has long been associated with graduate-level training and qualifications. The introduction of EYPS has given professional status to the early years workforce; however, the government's vision is to have a graduate leading practice across the whole children's workforce. Many of the different sectors of the workforce now require graduate-level qualifications – see Table 9.3 for examples.

Table 9.3 Job roles with relevant entry requirements

Job role	Entry requirements
Early years professional	Degree plus Early Years Professional Status
Teacher	Degree plus Qualified Teacher Status
Social worker	Degree level qualification
Professional youth worker	Degree which has been validated by the National Youth Agency
Nursing (including children's nurse)	From 2013 all those wishing to enter the nursing profession must be educated to degree level
Play therapist	Degree-level qualification plus postgraduate training

Please note that at the time of writing the EYPS is under review and will be replaced by the new early years teacher.

In Chapter 1 we discussed the common core of skills and knowledge (CCSK) required by all practitioners working within the children's workforce. Within some chapters we have referred back to the CCSK and asked you to identify areas for further development. Return now to your personal development plan (see Table 9.4) and identify the skills and knowledge that you need to acquire in order to become a confident and competent practitioner. Additionally, if you are much clearer about the direction you would like your career to take, consider any additional training and development you will need to undertake to ensure that you reach your goal.

Table 9.4 Personal development plan

Area of expertise	What do I need to learn?	How will this be achieved?	Resources required	Evidence of achievement	Target date
Effective communication					
Child and young person's development					
Safeguarding and promoting the welfare of the child					
Supporting transitions					
Multi-agency working					
Information sharing					

CHAPTER SUMMARY

In this chapter we explored the difference between leadership and management, concluding that they were two separate but complementary functions which were equally important to ensure that early years settings were sustainable and offered high-quality provision. We also explored the notion that leadership within early years settings can be distributed across the early years team, by assigning particular roles and responsibilities to staff. However, it must be acknowledged that for Ofsted purposes one person will ultimately be accountable for the setting, the registered named person, who is usually the nursery manager. Throughout the discussions we have linked leadership practices to the EYP standards and QTS standards specifically in relation to leading learning, and have reflected upon the influence that our leadership style has upon children's learning. Above all else, if as aspiring leaders we want to take our practice further, we cannot underestimate the value and importance of continuous professional development as a tool to improve our practice and to further our own careers. Becoming a practitioner in the early years is only the beginning!

Self-assessment questions

1. As leaders of learning we must undertake several tasks to ensure that children's individual needs are met. What are those tasks?
2. What are the three leadership styles identified and how do they influence children's learning?
3. What process ensures that children's learning and development is child-centred?

FURTHER READING

DfE (2012) *Teachers' Standards*. London: DfE Publications.

Stephen, C (2010) Pedagogy: the silent partner in early years, *Early Years*, 30 (1): 15–28. Available at: http://dx.doi.org/10.1080/09575140903402881.

Self-assessment answers

Chapter 1

Question 1
The Core Children's Workforce identifies all those whose primary role is to work directly with children and contribute to improving outcomes for them. The wider children's workforce identifies those who may not necessarily work directly with children and young people as part of their primary role, but their role contributes to improving outcomes for children and young people.

Question 2
The latest statistics concerning the number of lone parents with dependent children in the UK reveal an increase in the number of female lone parents with dependent children. In 2011, 92% of lone parents with dependent children were female, compared to only 8% of male lone parents with dependent children (National Office for Statistics, 2012), therefore there are a greater percentage of female lone parents with dependent children than male lone parents.

Question 3
The issues which may impact upon the recruitment of practitioners from BME groups include:

- Cultural differences relating to family expectations, that is Fatima required the approval of her husband before enrolling on the programme
- Language barriers which may result in communication difficulties
- Religious beliefs.

Chapter 2

Question 1
Effective communication, inter-agency trust and information sharing between agencies.

Question 2
The service model of partnership working, the systemic medical model of partnership working and collaborative models of partnership working.

Question 3
Strengths and weakness associated with the three models of partnership working are identified in the table below.

	Service model	Systemic medical model	Collaborative model
Strength	Ensures that the correct systems are in place to enable information to be shared between agencies where appropriate	Child- and family-focused	Promotes collaboration and communication between agencies to ensure services meet the needs of children and families
Weakness	The focus of this model is upon systems and protocols rather than upon the individual needs of families	There is little scope for children and families to be involved in the decision-making process	Dependent upon the commitment of all agencies to meet regularly and engage in the partnership

Chapter 3

Question 1

Throughout the chapter we have considered the theoretical aspects of play that encompass the 0–8 age range alongside the early years curriculum in England that focuses on children between the ages of 0–5. The theoretical perspective focuses on a play-based curriculum for children up to the age of 8, whereas the EYFS promotes the increase of structured, adult-guided play to support children in the transition into year 1 at five years of age – when they begin a more structured and formal focus to their learning. This can create, in the view of some, a potential tension between a pedagogy based on the promotion of free, sustained play and the requirements of the curriculum for regular summative assessments.

Question 2

Play, as discussed within this chapter is difficult to define. Play in its broadest sense is focused on children's opportunities to choose play for themselves, manage the direction of the play and make choices in their play. This type of play is relating to children's general experiences of play, rather than the types of play that is developed in a nursery and school situation, when the opportunities to direct and manage their own play can be more directed through a practitioner.

Question 3

a) Children define activities as playful when they involve an element of choice, the ability to move around and, ideally, don't include adults at all – and certainly not in any way that evaluates their involvement. This latter point, of course, is not possible in a teaching environment, but play can be enhanced by adults taking part on an equal basis. Whatever activities you came up with in answer to this question should be considered in light of this.

b) Piaget – A typical approach to play starting from Piaget's ideas could be providing resources that enable exploration and construction in an independent way. Practitioners will often set up parts of the early years environment with this particularly in mind so that when children play in the set areas of the environment they are able to do so in a way that follows their own interests.

c) Vygotsky – Vygotsky was concerned with the child working within the zone of proximal development with the support of a more able other. This is reflected in activities that have been specifically planned by a practitioner to develop a child's learning in a particular area of learning with the intention of supporting them initially – which will then enable them to have a go at the activity independently at a later stage.

Chapter 4

Question 1
Past experiences, present experience, our childhood and our education.

Question 2
Schemas are patterns of repeatable behaviour that can be noticed in children's play and can illustrate their combining of thinking and exploration. Schemas follow the child's interest.

Question 3
A constructivist approach to learning is based on the assumption that we make meaning of the world through our first-hand experience of the environment. It is based on the belief that we are actively involved in a process of learning and as learners we construct knowledge and meaning for ourselves through this process – and in a strong sense, 'invent the world'.

Chapter 5

Question 1
Observation takes many different forms and the key to successful observation is to be clear about the purpose and nature of the observation. Much of the observations will be used to enable you to assess the level/stage a child is working at to enable you to plan activities through running records or learning journeys and checklist. There will also be situations when you need to focus and observe a child to identify types of behaviour, for example, a child who is biting other children. For this type of observation it would be appropriate to use event sampling in which the practitioner watches for incidents of biting and writes down everything before and following the biting incident to try and address causes and effects and address the behaviours. Using observations to successfully support the growth, learning and development of children, it is important to develop your knowledge and understanding of the different types of observations to enable you to make informed decisions on the appropriate form to support children. The key then is to reflect on the observations in a purposeful way in order to enable them to be used to support the needs and development of the children.

Question 2
The very language of play-based and outcome-driven curriculum can sit in tension with some of the research and understanding of play as discussed in Chapter 5.

Implementing a play-based curriculum can create a tension for practitioners when you consider play in relation to statutory curriculum guidance. The EYFS gives us early learning goals that children are expected to reach in their final term in reception, yet when we look at indicators of good-quality play this is concerned with children making choices and having the ability to control the direction of their play. When you begin to align this with child-directed play and adult-structured play we need to ensure we develop a balance that enables children to have control and direct their play, while enabling you as a practitioner to step in and enhance this through careful questioning and modeling. This can at times be a difficult balance to achieve.

Chapter 6

Question 1
The purpose of reflective practice is to enhance and develop our practice for us as a practitioner, but also to help the children we are working with. For practitioners reflective practice supports us in evaluating our work and helps us to make choices in order to support and develop future situations. Children are at the heart of the reflective practice process, as they are the focus – for the development and enhancement of learning experiences to create stronger learning opportunities.

Question 2
Reflective practice is a learned process and it takes time and practice to engage in a deep and meaningful process of reflection. Time is something that is generally not in abundance for practitioners working in early years, but is needed to enable you to work through the different stages of an incident or activity. This will allow you to look with an honest and critical eye to enable you to develop and change your practice if necessary. Reflective practice is a tool for enhancing your practice, therefore, it is important that you are looking for strengths and areas to develop and not using it to simply criticise your practice. It is about developing change for the better (see section on criticisms of reflective practice, page 91).

Chapter 7

Question 1
Segregation within a mainstream school is the act of taking children out of their class to be taught separately, whereas integration is about making limited number of additional arrangements for individual pupils with SEN in schools to enable the child to fit in with the school. A fully inclusive school or early years setting is one which adapts to the needs of all children and ensures that *all* children have their individual needs met whatever their circumstance, so that they can achieve their full potential, therefore the onus is upon the school to change and adapt to be responsive to the needs of all children so that they receive their education in the same class as their peers.

Question 2

Strengths and weaknesses associated with the three models to promote inclusive practice are identified in the table below.

	The psycho-medical model	The social model of disability	The rights-based model of disability
Strength	The individual needs of children are met, albeit as a result of the diagnosis of the disability	Advocates that if society removed all barriers to learning full inclusion would be possible	Promotes full inclusion for all children
Weakness	Ignores societal influences in which people live	Does not take into account the holistic nature of SEN and Disability	It could take a long time to bring about legislative changes

Question 3

The four elements of inclusive practice are: accessible, i.e. they provide a range of play and learning activities for all children; foster participation by accommodating the needs of individual children whatever their circumstance; are supportive and have in place the necessary systems and processes to ensure children's needs are met; and enable all children to achieve their full potential.

Chapter 8

Question 1

Staff need to follow the physical and health requirements set out in the EYFS Safeguarding & Welfare Requirements (DfE, 2012b) to ensure the safety and security of buildings and equipment, prevent infection, administer medicines safely and obtain emergency medical treatment where necessary. They also require settings to ensure children's emotional well-being by managing behaviour appropriately and assigning each child a 'key person'.

Settings need to follow safe recruitment guidance when employing staff, and pass any allegations or concerns about any member of staff having posed a risk of harm to a child to the LADO, Ofsted and the Disclosure & Barring Service. Managers need to foster open and supportive communication at all levels so that a 'zero threshold' applies, so that both staff and parents can raise even small concerns. Having a 'range of listening systems' for children is also beneficial. Building resilience in children through positive behaviour management techniques, active listening to children, allowing them to make choices, and helping children make and maintain friendships are all important.

Question 2

Processes	What can be done to counteract these
Lack of awareness of the signs/symptoms of possible abuse and neglect	Undertake good-quality safeguarding training, and update this regularly
Resistance to accepting disturbing information – repression and rationalisation	Awareness of these processes helps – then attempting to be self-reflective and questioning in your interpretation of what you see is helpful Ensure that even minor concerns can be shared with the manager or 'Designated Person' for safeguarding is helpful (a 'zero threshold' approach)
'Selective attention' – where we are unaware of events outside our current focus of attention	Check: 'Have I missed anything?' Ensure supervision and team discussions are prioritised so perceptions are shared within the team
'Change blindness' – where we fail to see changes in detail over time	

Question 3
Refer back to Table 8.1 (Disorganised attachment behaviours).

Chapter 9

Question 1
Observation and assessment, planning, evaluation, communicating with children and their parents.

Question 2
The three leaderships styles identified are: autocratic, democratic and laissez-faire.

Autocratic leaders stifle children's learning insofar as, children are not given the opportunity to think for themselves, that is, the autocratic leader dictates what activities will be done and how these will be carried out, therefore children are not encouraged to be creative.

Democratic leadership fosters an ethos of mutual respect between children and practitioners. Children's interests are taken into consideration during the planning process, they are allowed to be creative when carrying out tasks.

Laissez-faire leaders do not take ownership of the planning therefore there is a risk that planning will be inconsistent. There is also a risk that play will not be purposive as is required within EYFS, that is, all activities will be child-initiated and perhaps not supported by a practitioner, as a result children's learning may not be progressed or activities may not be extended.

Question 3
The process which ensures that children's learning and development is child-centred is Sustained Shared Thinking (SST). Practitioners engage in SST by being involved in meaningful interactions with children, and working together collaboratively to ensure that children are equally involved in the interactions.

Practitioners must be aware of the child's interests and be able to follow their interest to enable children develop their ideas or to solve a problem.

References

Ainscow, M (1999) *Understanding the Development of Inclusive Schools*. London: Falmer.

Ainscow, M (2007) Taking an inclusive turn, *Journal of Research in Special Educational Needs*, 1 (1): 3–7.

Ainsworth, M, Blehar, M, Walters, E and Wall, S (1978) *Patterns of Attachment*. Hillsdale, NJ: Erlbaum.

Alakeson, V (2004) *A 2020 Vision for Early Years: Extending Choice, Improving life Chances*. London: Social Market Foundation.

Alexander, R (2001) *Culture and Pedagogy: International Comparisons in Primary Education*. London: Blackwell.

Alexander, R (2004) Still no pedagogy? Principle, pragmatism and compliance in primary education, *Cambridge Journal of Education*, 34 (1): 7–33.

Allen, G (2011a) *Early Intervention: The Next Steps*. London: Cabinet Office.

Allen, G (2011b) *Early Intervention: Smart Investment, Massive Savings*. London: Cabinet Office.

Allen, S and Whalley, M (2010) *Supporting Pedagogy and Practice in Early Years Settings*. Exeter: Learning Matters.

Allnock, D with Bunting, L, Price, A, Morgan-Klein, N, Ellis, J, Radford, L and Stafford, A (2009) *Sexual Abuse and Therapeutic Services for Children and Young People*. London: NSPCC. Available at: www.nspcc.org.uk/Inform/research/findings/sexual_abuse_therapeutic_services_summary_wdf67005.pdf (accessed 6 September 2012).

Arblaster, L, Conway, L, Foreman, A and Howtin, M (1996) *Setting Us Up to Fail? A Study of Interagency Working to Address Housing, Health, and Social Care Needs of People in General Needs Housing*. York: Joseph Rowntree Foundation.

Asch, SE (1955) Opinions and social pressure, *Scientific American*, 193: 31–5.

Athey, C (2007) *Extending Thought in Young Children: A Parent–Teacher Partnership*, 2nd edn. London: Paul Chapman.

Audit Commission (1998) *A Fruitful Partnership*. London: Audit Commission.

Bakermans-Kranenberg, MJ, van IJzendoorn, MH and Juffer, F (2005) Disorganised infant attachment and preventative interventions: a review and meta-analysis, *Infant Mental Health Journal*, 26: 191–216.

Ball, C (1994) *Start Right: The Importance of Early Learning*. London: Royal Society for the Encouragement of Arts, Manufactures & Commerce.

Balloch, S and Taylor, M (2001) *Partnership Working*. Bristol: Policy Press.

Barlow, J, Schrader-McMillan, A, Kirkpatrick, S, Ghate, D, Smith, M and Barnes, J (2008) *Health-led Parenting Interventions in Pregnancy and Early Years*. Nottingham: DCSF.

Bertram, T and Pascal, C (2002) *Early Years Education: An International Perspective*. London: Qualifications and Curriculum Authority.

Birmingham Safeguarding Children Board (2010) *Serious Case Review in Respect of the Death of a Child – Case Number 14*. Birmingham: Birmingham SCB. Available at: **www.lscbbirmingham.org.uk/downloads/ Case+14.pdf** (accessed 15 August 2012).

Blandford, S and Knowles, C (2009) *Developing Professional Practice 0–7*. Harlow: Pearsons.

Blewett, J (2007) The challenge for partnerships, *Community Care*, 1683: 28–9.

Boffey, D and McVeigh, T (2012) Leak reveals benefits cap will hit 100,000 children, *Observer*, 22 January, p14.

Boud, D, Keogh, R and Walker, D (1985) *Reflection: Turning Experience into Learning*. London: Kogan Page.

Brandon, M, Sidebotham, P, Bailey, S, Belderson, P, Hawley, C, Ellis C and Megson, M (2012) *New Learning from Serious Case Reviews: A Two Year Report for 2009–2011*. London: DfE. Available at: **https:// www.education.gov.uk/publications/standard/publicationDetail/Page1/DFE-RR226** (accessed 1 September 2012).

Bratton, SC, Ray, D, Rhine, T and Jones, L (2005) The efficacy of play therapy with children: a meta-analytic review of treatment outcomes, *Professional Psychology: Research and Practice*, 36(4): 376–90.

Broadhead, P, Howard, J and Wood, E (eds) (2010) *Play and Learning in the Early Years, from Research to Practice*. London: Sage.

Brooker, L and Edwards, S (2010) *Engaging Play*. Maidenhead: Open University Press.

Brookfield, SD (1987) *Developing Critical Thinkers: Challenging Adults to Explore Alternative Ways of Thinking and Acting*. San Francisco: Jossey-Bass

Brookfield, SD (1995) *Becoming a Critically Reflective Teacher*. San Francisco: Jossey-Bass.

Browne, J (2012) *The Impact of Austerity Measures on Households with Children*. London: Family and Parenting Institute.

Bruce, T (2001) *Learning Through Play: Babies, Toddlers and the Foundation Years*. Abingdon: Hodder & Stoughton.

Bruce, T (2004) *Developing Learning in Early Childhood 0–8*. London: Paul Chapman.

Bruce, T (ed.) (2006) *Early Childhood: A Guide for Students*. London: Sage.

Bunting, M (2011) Tough love for troubled families, *Guardian*, 9 February. Available at: **www.guardian.co.uk/ society/2011/feb/09/tough-love-troubled-families-swindon-participle** (accessed 6 September 2012).

Butler, P (2013) Hundreds of Sure Start centres have closed since election, says Labour, The Guardian, 28 January. Available at **www.guardian.co.uk/society/2013/jan/28/sure-start-centres-closed-labour** (accessed 6 March 2013).

C4EO and WAVE Trust (2010) *International Experience of Early Intervention for Children, Young People and Their Families*. Available at: **www.c4eo.org.uk/themes/earlyintervention/files/ early_intervention_wave_trust_international_desk_study.pdf** (accessed 14 September 2012).

Canning, N (2011) *Play and Practice in the Early Years Foundation Stage*. London: Sage.

Cate, D, Diefondorf, M, McCullough, K, Peters, ML and Whaley, K (eds) (2010) *Quality Indicators of Inclusive Practice Early Childhood Programmes/Practices: A Compilation of Selected Resources*. Chapel Hill, NC: University of North Carolina, FPG Child Development Institute, National Early Childhood Technical Assistance Center.

Cawson, P, Wattam, C, Brooker, S and Kelly, G (2000) *Child Maltreatment in the United Kingdom: A Study of the Prevalence of Child Abuse and Neglect*. London: NSPCC.

Cefai, C (2008) *Promoting Resilience in the Classroom*. London: Jessica Kingsley.

Chabris, C and Simons, D (2010a) *The Invisible Gorilla*. London: HarperCollins.

Chabris, C and Simons D (2010b) *The Invisible Gorilla*. Video. Available at: **www.theinvisiblegorilla.com/ gorilla_experiment.html** (accessed 24 August 2012).

Challen, A, Noden, P, West, A and Machine, S (2011) *UK Resilience Programme Evaluation: Final Report*. Runcorn: DfE.

Channing Bete (2012) *PATHS (Promoting Alternative Thinking Strategies)*. Program. Available at: **www.channing-bete.com/prevention-programs/paths/paths.html** (accessed 16 September 2012).

Chief Secretary to the Treasury (2003) *Every Child Matters*, CM 8650. London: Stationery Office.

Coleman, M (2005) Gender and educational leadership in England: a comparison of secondary headteacher's views over time, *School Leadership and Management* (formerly *School Organisation*), 27 (4): 383–99.

Costa, AL and Kallick, B (1993) Through the lens of a critical friend, *Educational Leadership*, 51 (2): 49–51.

CWDC (2009) *The Common Assessment Framework for Children and Young People: A Guide for Practitioners*. Leeds: DCSF Publications.

CWDC (2010) *The Common Core of Skills and Knowledge*. Leeds: DCSF Publications.

Darcer, A, Baltodano, M and Torres, RD (eds) (2003) *The Critical Pedagogy Reader*. London: RoutledgeFalmer.

Dawson, S (2007) Interprofessional working: communication, collaboration . . . perspiration!', *International Journal of Palliative Nursing*, 13 (10): 502–5.

Daycare Trust (2003) *Men and Childcare*. Available at: **http://www.mori.com/polls/2003/ Daycaretrust2003.shtml** (accessed on 22 May 2012).

Department for Children, Schools and Families (2008a) *Statutory Framework for the Early Learning Foundation Stage: Setting the Standards for Learning, Development and Care for Children from Birth to Five*. Nottingham: DCFS Publications.

Department for Children, Schools and Families (2008b) *Building Brighter Futures: Next Steps for the Children's Workforce*. Nottingham: DCSF Publications.

Department for Children, Schools and Families (2008c) *Staying Safe Action Plan*. Nottingham: DCSF Publications.

Department for Children, Schools and Families (2008d) *Information Sharing: Guidance for Practitioners and Managers*. Nottingham: DCSF Publications.

Department for Children, Schools and Families (2008e) *2020 Children and Young People's Workforce Strategy*. Nottingham: DCSF Publications.

Department for Children, Schools and Families (2009a) *Learning, Playing and Interacting: Good Practice in the Early Years Foundation Stage*. Nottingham: DCSF Publications.

Department for Children, Schools and Families (2009b) *Understanding Serious Case Reviews and Their Impact – A Biennial Analysis of Serious Case Reviews 2005–2007*. London: DCSF.

Department for Education (2010a) *Childcare and early years provider survey* (2010) Cheshire: DfE.

Department for Education (2010b) *Improving Outcomes for Gypsy, Roma and Traveller Pupils: Final Report*. Nottingham: National Foundation for Educational Research.

Department for Education (2011a) *Review of the Early Years Foundation Stage: Report on the Evidence*.

Available at: **http://media.education.gov.uk/assets/Files/pdf/T/The%20Tickell%20Review.pdf** accessed on 28 June 2012).

Department for Education (2011b) *Number of Children's Centres by Local Authority*. Cheshire: DfE. Available at: **www.education.gov.uk/inthenews/inthenews/a00200125/number-of-childrens-centres-by-local-authority** (accessed 17 September 2012).

Department for Education (2011c) *Supporting Families in the Foundation Years*. Cheshire: DfE.

Department for Education (2011d) *Number of Children's Centres by Local Authority*. Cheshire: DfE. Available at: **www.education.gov.uk/inthenews/inthenews/a00200125/number-of-childrens-centres-by-local-authority** (accessed: 17 September 2012).

Department for Education (2012a) *Men into Childcare*. Available at: **www.education.gov.uk/inthenews/inthenews/a00211812/record-numbers-of-men-teaching-in-primary-schools** (accessed 17 July 2012).

Department for Education (2012b) *Statutory Framework for the Early Years Foundation Stage: Setting the Standards for Learning, Development and Care for Children from Birth to Five*. London: DfE.

Department for Education (2012c) *Teachers' Standards*. London: DfE Publications.

Department for Education (2012d) *EYPS Standards*. Available at: **www.education.gov.uk/publications/eOrderingDownload/eyps%20standards%20from%20september%202012.pdf** (accessed on 10 August 2012).

Department for Education (2013) *More Great Childcare. Raising quality and giving parents more choice*. London: DFE.

Department for Education and Department of Health (2011) *Supporting Children in the Foundation Years*. London: HMSO.

Department for Education and Employment (1997) *Excellence for All Children: Meeting Special Educational Needs*, Green Paper, 22 October. London: HMSO.

Department for Education and Employment (1998) *The National Childcare Strategy: Meeting the Childcare Challenge*. London: HMSO.

Department for Education and Employment and School Curriculum and Assessment Authority (1996) *Desirable Outcomes for Children's Learning on Entering Compulsory Education*. London: DfEE.

Department for Education and Skills (2001) *Special Educational Needs Code of Practice*. London: HMSO.

Department for Education and Skills (2002) *Birth to Three Matters: A Framework to Support Children in Their Earliest Years*. London: DfES.

Department for Education and Skills (2003) *Every Child Matters*. London: DfES.

Department for Education and Skills (2004a) *Every Child Matters: Change for Children*. London: HMSO.

Department for Education and Skills (2004b) *Ten-Year Childcare Strategy: Choice for Parents. The Best Start for Children*. London: HMSO.

Department for Education and Skills (2005a) *Children's Workforce Strategy*. Nottingham: DfES Publications.

Department for Education and Skills (2005b) *Key Elements of Effective Practice*. London: DfES.

Department for Education and Skills (2006a) *What to Do If You Are Worried a Child Is Being Abused – Summary*. Nottingham: DfES Publications. Available at: **https://www.education.gov.uk/publications/standard/_arc_SOP/Page21/DFES-04319-2006**.

Department for Education and Skills (2006b) *Safeguarding Children and Safer Recruitment in Education*. Nottingham: DfES.

Department of Health (1995) *Child Protection: Messages from Research*. London: HMSO.

Department of Health (2011) *Health and Social Care Bill*. London: Stationary Office.

Department of Health (2012a) *Health Visitor Implementation Plan: Quarterly Progress Report April–June 2012*. London: DoH. Available at: **www.dh.gov.uk/health/2012/07/health-visitors/** (accessed 17 September 2012).

Department of Health (2012b) *Family Nurse Partnership Programme Information Leaflet*. London: DoH. Available at: **www.dh.gov.uk/health/2012/07/family-nurse-partnership-programme-information-leaflet/** (accessed 17 September 2012).

Dewey, J (1910) *How We Think*. New York: DC Heath.

Donaldson, J and Scheffler, A (1999) *The Gruffalo*. London: Macmillan.

Doyle, J (2008) Barriers and facilitators of multidisciplinary team working: a review, *Journal of Paediatric Nursing*, 20 (2): 26–9.

Driscoll, J and Teh, B (2001) The potential of reflective practice to develop individual orthopaedic nurse practitioners and their practice, *Journal of Orthopaedic Nursing*, 5 (2): 95–103.

Drummond, MJ (1993) *Assessing Young Children's Learning*. London: David Fulton.

Dunnell, K (2007) The Changing Demographic Picture of the UK: National Statistician's Annual Article 'The Population'. Available at: **www.statistics.gov.uk/hub/population/index.html** (accessed on 30 June 2012).

Eaude, T (2011) *Thinking Through Pedagogy for Primary and Early Years*. Exeter: Learning Matters.

Edmond, N and Price, M (2007) *The Emergence of New 'Professional' and 'Associate Professional' Roles in the Children's Workforce – A Rhetorical Device or a New Model of Professionalism*. Available at: **www.leeds.ac.uk/medicine/meu/lifelong07/Nadia_Edmond_and_Mark_Price.pdf** (accessed 30 October 2012).

Edwards, A (2004) The new multi-agency working: collaborating to prevent social inclusion of children and families, *Journal of Integrated Care*, 12 (5): 3–9.

Ennals, P (2012) Do they still want us to 'work together'? *Children and Young People Now*, 4 September, pp18–19.

Erooga, M (2009) *Towards Safer Organisations*. London: NSPCC.

Every Child in Need (2012) *Response of the Every Child in Need Campaign to the Department for Education's Consultation on 'Revised Safeguarding Statutory Guidance'*. Available at: **www.everychildinneed.org.uk/app/download/5797160754/ECIN+Consultation+Response.pdf** (accessed 16 September 2012).

Fan, XT and Chen, M (2001) Parent involvement and students' academic achievement: a meta-analysis, *Educational Psychology Review*, 13: 1–22.

Fisher, PA, Burraston, B and Pears, K (2005) The Early Intervention Foster Care Program: permanent placement outcomes from a randomized trial, *Child Maltreatment*; 10 (1): 61–71.

Fukkink, RG and Lont, A (2007) Does training matter? A meta-analysis and review of caregiver training studies, *Early Childhood Research Quarterly*, 22: 294–311.

Gardner, R (2008) *Developing an Effective Response to Neglect and Emotional Harm to Children*. Norwich: UEA/NSPCC.

Gibbs, G (1988) *Learning by Doing: A Guide to Teaching and Learning Methods.* Oxford: Further Educational Unit, Oxford Polytechnic.

Gibbs, G (1998) *Learning by Doing: A Guide to Teaching and Learning.* London: FEU.

Glaister, A and Glaister, B (2005) *Inter-Agency Collaboration – Providing for Children*. Edinburgh: Dunedin Academic Press.

Goodman, S and Trowler, I (2012) *Social Work Reclaimed*. London: Jessica Kingsley.

Greco, V and Sloper, P (2004) Care co-ordination and key worker schemes for disabled children: results of a UK wide survey, *Childcare Health and Development*, 30: 13–20.

Hall, K, Murphy, P and Soler, J (2008) *Pedagogy and Practice, Culture and Identities*. London: Sage.

Higgs, L (2012) Terrifying welfare reforms will drive up care referrals, *Children and Young People Now*, 6 July.

HM Government (2002) *Education Act*. London: TSO.

HM Government (2004) *Children Act*. London: TSO.

HM Government (2006) *Childcare Act*. London: TSO.

HM Government (2008) *Information Sharing Guidance for Managers and Practitioners*. London: DCSF Publications.

HM Government (2009) *Apprenticeship, Skills and Learning Act*. Available at: **www.legislation.gov.uk/ukpga/2009/22/pdfs/ukpga_20090022_en.pdf** (accessed 23 February 2012).

HM Government (2010) *Equality Act*. London: TSO.

Holmes, E (1912) *What Is and What Might Be?* London: Constable.

House, R (ed.) (2011) *Too Much Too Soon: Early Learning and the Erosion of Childhood*. Gloucestershire: Hawthorn Press.

Hughes, B and Paterson, K (1997) The social model of disability and the disappearing body: towards a sociology of impairment, *Disability and Society*, 12 (3): 325–40.

Jackson, L (2012) *Securing Standards, Sustaining Success*. National Education Trust. Available at: **www.cypnow.co.uk/digital_assets//EarlyYearsReport.pdf** (accessed 10 September 2012).

Janis, IL (1982) *Groupthink: Psychological Studies of Policy Decisions and Fiascos*, 2nd edn. New York: Houghton Mifflin.

Jasper, M (2003) *Becoming a Reflective Practitioner: Foundations in Nursing and Health*. Cheltenham: Nelson Thornes.

Jigsaw (2009) *Has a Child Been Sexually Abused?* Available at: **http://bit.ly/UT2We8** (accessed 14 September 2012).

Johns, C (2002) *Guided Reflection: Advancing Practice*. Oxford: Blackwell.

Johns, C (2009) *Becoming a Reflective Practitioner*, 3rd edn. Oxford: Blackwell.

Johnston, J and Nahmad-Williams, L (2009) *Early Childhood Studies*. Harlow: Pearson Longman.

Jozwiak, G (2012) Two-year-old entitlement to be funded by cut to early intervention grant, *Children and Young People Now*. Available at: **www.cypnow.co.uk/cyp/news/1074769/two-entitlement-funded-cut-intervention-grant** (accessed 3 January 2013).

Kalinauskiene, L, Cekuoliene, D, Van IJzendoorn, MH, Bakermans-Kranenberg, MJ, Juffer, E and Kidscape (2009) *Keep Them Safe!* London: Kidscape. Available at: **www.kidscape.org.uk/assets/downloads/kskeepthemsafe.pdf** (accessed 16 September 2012).

Kenworthy, J and Whittaker, J (2000) Anything to declare? The struggle for inclusive education and children's rights, *Disability and Society*, 15 (2): 219–31.

Kidscape (2007) *Keep Them Safe!* London: Kidscape Available at: **http://www.kidscape.org.uk/assets/ downloads/kskeepthemsafe.pdf** (accessed on 16 September 2012).

Kolb, DA (1984) *Experiential Learning: Experiences as the Source of Learning and Development.* London: Prentice Hall.

Kozulin, A, Gindis, B, Ageyev, VS and Miller, SM (2003) *Vygotsky's Educational Theory in Cultural Context.* Cambridge: Cambridge University Press.

Krasnor, LR and Pepler, DJ (1980) The study of children's play: some suggested future directions, in Rubin, KH (ed.), *New Directions for Child Development: Children's Play.* San Francisco: Jossey-Bass, pp89–95.

Kusakovskaja, I (2009) Supporting insensitive mothers, *Child: Care, Health and Development,* 35 (5): 613–23.

Laming, H (2003) *The Victoria Climbié Inquiry Report.* London: HMSO.

Laming, H (2009) *The Protection of Children in England: A Progress Report.* London: Stationery Office

Leach, J and Moon, B (eds) (1999) *Learners and Pedagogy.* London: Paul Chapman.

Leach, J and Moon, B (2008) *The Power of Pedagogy.* London: Sage.

Leadbetter, J, Morris, S, Timmins, P, Knight, G and Traxson, D (1999) *Applying Psychology in the Classroom.* Oxon: David Fulton .

Lester, H, Birtchwood, M, Tait, L, Shah, S, England, E and Smith, J (2008) Barriers and facilitators to partnership working between early intervention services and the voluntary community sector, *Health and Social Care in the Community,* 16 (5): 493–500.

Lewin, K (1939) Experiments in social space, in Gentle, BF and Miller, BO (eds) (2009) *Foundations of Psychological Thought: A History of Psychology.* London: Sage.

Life (2012) *Professionals: A Different Way of Working.* Available at: **www.alifewewant.com/display/HOME/ Professionals** (accessed 6 September 2012).

Lindon, J (2007) *Understanding Child Development: Linking Theory and Practice.* London: Hodder Arnold.

Local Government Association (2012) *Revised Safeguarding Statutory Guidance Consultation – Working Together to Safeguard Children.* Available at: **www.local.gov.uk/web/guest/safeguarding-children/-/ journal_content/56/10171/3702837/ARTICLE-TEMPLATE** (accessed 15 September 2012).

Loughran, JJ (1996) *Developing Reflective Practice: Learning About Teaching and Learning Through Modeling.* Washington, DC: Falmer.

Macleod-Brudenell, I and Kay, J (eds) (2008) *Advanced Early Years for Foundation Degrees and Levels 4/5,* 2nd edn. Harlow: Heinemann.

MacMillan, HL (2010) *Research Brief: Interventions to Prevent Child Maltreatment.* London: PreVAiL: Preventing Violence Across the Lifespan Research Network. Available at: **http://prevail.fims.uwo.ca/docs/ CM%20Research%20Brief%20Mar10.pdf** (accessed: 6 September 2012)

MacMillan, HL, Wathen, CN, Barlow, J, Fergusson, DM, Levethal, JM and Taussig, HN (2009) Interventions to prevent child maltreatment and associated impairment, *The Lancet,* 373: 250–66.

Mahadevan, J (2012) Pioneering free childcare scheme in Kirklees bids to get families into work. *Children and Young People Now,* 4–17 September.

Marton, F, Watkins, D and Tang, C (1997) Discontinuities and continuities in the experience of learning: an interview study of high school students in Hong Kong, *Learning and Instruction,* 7 (1): 21–48.

Masten, AS, Best, KM and Garmezy, N (1990) Resilience and development: contributions from the study of children who overcame adversity, *Development and Psychopathology*, 2 (4): 425–44.

Miller, C and Cable, C (2011) *Professionalization, Leadership and Management in the Early Years.* London: Sage.

Miller, L (2008) 'Developing professionalism within a regulatory framework in England: challenges and possibilities', *European Early Childhood Education Research Journal*, 16 (2): 255–68.

Mindes, G (2011) *Assessing Young Children*, 4th edn. Boston: Pearson.

Moon, JA (2001) *A Handbook of Reflective and Experiential Learning: Theory and Practice*. Abingdon: RoutldgeFalmer.

Moon, J (2002) *The Module and Programme Development Handbook*. London: Kogan Page.

Moon, J (2004) *A Handbook of Reflective and Experiential Learning: Theory and Practice*. Abingdon: RoutledgeFalmer.

Moon, J (2006) *Learning Journals: A Handbook for Reflective Practice and Professional Development*. Abingdon: Routledge

Moran, P (2006) Multi-agency working: implications for an early-intervention social work team, *Child and Family Social Work*, 12: 143–51.

Morrison, GS (2011) *Fundamentals of Early Childhood Education*. New York: Pearson.

Mortimer, J, North, M, Katz, A and Stead, J (2012) *You Have Someone to Trust: Outstanding Safeguarding Practice in Primary Schools*. London: Office of the Children's Commissioner – report on a study of best practice in safeguarding in primary schools.

Moyles, JR (1989) *Just Playing? The Role and Status of Play in Early Childhood Education*. Milton Keynes: Open University Press.

Moyles, JR (ed.) (2005) *The Excellence of Play*, 2nd edn. Maidenhead: Open University Press.

Moyles, JR (2010) *The Excellence of Play*, 3rd edn. Maidenhead: Open University Press.

Moyles, J, Adams, S and Musgrove, A (2002) *A Study of Pedagogical Effectiveness in Early Learning.* Northwich: DfES Publications

Munro, E (2011a) *The Munro Review of Child Protection: Interim Report – The Child's Journey*. London, DfE. Available at: **www.education.gov.uk/munroreview/downloads/Munrointerimreport.pdf**.

Munro, E (2011b) *The Munro Review of Child Protection: Final Report - A Child-Centred System*. London: DfE. Available at: **www.education.gov.uk/munroreview/downloads/8875_DfE_Munro_Report_TAGGED.pdf**.

Munro, E (2012) *Progress Report: Moving Towards a Child-Centred System*. Available at: **https://www.education.gov.uk/publications/standard/Childrenandfamilies/Page1/DFE-00063-2012** (accessed 10 September 2012).

Munton, T, Mooney, A, Moss, P, Petre, P, Clark, A and Woolner, J (2002) *Research on Ratios, Group Size and Staff Qualifications in Early Years and Childcare Settings.* Norwich: DfES Publications.

NatCen (2010) *ASB Family Intervention Projects*. London: DCSF Publications.

National Institute for Clinical Excellence (2005) *Post Traumatic Stress Disorder*, National Clinical Practice Guideline No. 26. Available at: **www.nice.org.uk/nicemedia/live/10966/29772/29772.pdf** (accessed 6 September 2012).

National Office for Statistics (2012) Available at: **http://www.ons.gov.uk/ons/rel/family-demography/families-and-households/2012/index.html** (accessed 22 May 2012).

Neaum, S (2013) *Child Development for Early Years Students and Practitioners*. Exeter: Learning Matters.

North Somerset Safeguarding Children Board (2012) *Serious Case Review: The Sexual Abuse of Pupils in a First School – Overview Report*. Somerset: North Somerset SCB. Available at: **www.northsomersetlscb.org.uk/ uploads/files/282.pdf** (accessed 15 August 2012).

NSPCC (2011) *NSPCC Report and Accounts 2010/11*.London: NSPCC. Available at: **www.nspcc.org.uk/what-we-do/about-the-nspcc/annual-report/annual-report-2011/annual-review-2010_wdf84903.pdf** (accessed 21 August 2012).

NSPCC (2012) Core Info series. Available at: **www.nspcc.org.uk/core-info** (accessed 14 September 2012).

NSPCC (no date) *Neglect*. Available at: **http://bit.ly/Qp3Lsx** (accessed 14 September 2012).

Nutbrown, C (1996) *Respectful Educators: Capable Learners – Children's Rights in the Early Years*. London: Paul Chapman.

Nutbrown, C (2012) *Foundations for Quality: Independent Review of Early Education and Childcare Qualifications, Final Report.* London: DfE Publications.

Nutbrown, C, Clough, P and Selbie, P (2008) *Early Childhood Education: History, Philosophy and Experience*. London: Sage.

Office of the Children's Commissioner (2012) *Practical Tips for Schools from the Report: You Have Someone to Trust – Outstanding Safeguarding Practice in Primary Schools*. London: Office of the Children's Commissioner.

Office for Standards in Education (2007) *OfSTED Departmental Report 2006–07*. London: Stationary Office.

Office for Standards in Education (2008) The Louisa Nursery. Report for early years provision. Available at **www.ofsted.gov.uk/inspection-reports/final-inspection-report/provider/CARE/EY360773**. (Accessed on 6 March 2012).

Office for Standards in Education (2010) *Learning Lessons from Serious Case Reviews 2009–10*. Manchester: Ofsted. Available at: **www.ofsted.gov.uk/resources/learning-lessons-serious-case-reviews-2009-2010** (accessed 15 August 2012)

Office for Standards in Education (2011a) *Inspection Report for Coundon Children's Centre*. Available at: **www.ofsted.gov.uk/inspection-reports/find-inspection-report/provider/ELS/20836** (accessed 6 March 2012).

Office for Standards in Education (2011b) *Annual Unannounced Inspection of Contact Referral and Assessment Arrangements within North Yorkshire County Council Children's Services*. Available at: **www.ofsted.gov.uk/sites/default/files/documents/local_authority_reports/north_yorkshire/ 003_Unannounced%20inspection%20as%20pdf.pdf** (accessed 31 August 2012).

Osgood, J (2009) Childcare workforce reform in England and 'the Early Years professional': a critical discourse analysis, *Journal of Education Policy*, 24 (6): 733–51.

Paige-Smith, A and Craft, A (2011) *Developing Reflective Practice in the Early Years*, 2nd edn. Maidenhead: McGraw-Hill.

Parten, M (1932) Social participation among preschool children, *Journal of Abnormal and Social Psychology*, 27: 243–69.

Peters, RS (1964) *Education as Initiation*. London: Institute of Education.

Piaget, J (1929) *The Child's Conception of the World*. London: Routledge & Kegan Paul.

Plowden, B (1967) *Children and Their Primary Schools: A Report of the Central Advisory Council for Education (England)*. London: HMSO.

Plymouth Safeguarding Children Board (2010) *Serious Case Review Overview Report: Executive Summary in Respect of Nursery Z, Plymouth*. Plymouth: Plymouth SCB. Available at: **www.plymouth.gov.uk/ serious_case_review_nursery_z.pdf** (accessed 15 August 2012).

Pound, L (2011) *Influencing Early Childhood Education*. Maidenhead: McGraw-Hill Open University Press.

Pritchard, C and Williams, R (2010) Comparing possible 'child-abuse-related-deaths' in England and Wales with the major developed countries 1974–2006: signs of progress? *British Journal of Social Work*, 40 (6): 1700–18.

Puffett, N (2010) Government clarifies ban on Every Child Matters, *Children and Young People Now*, 9 August. Available at: **www.cypnow.co.uk/cyp/news/1053008/government-clarifies-ban-every-child-matters** (accessed 14 September 2012).

Qualifications and Curriculum Authority (2000) *Curriculum Guidance for the Foundation Stage*. London: QCA.

Radford, L, Corral, S, Bradley, C, Fisher, H, Bassett, C, Howat, N and Collishaw, S (2011) *Child Abuse and Neglect in the UK Today*. London: NSPCC.

Ranns, H, Newmark, T, Rahim, N and Penfold, C (2011) *Evaluation of Graduate Leader Fund: GLF Implementation Case Studies*. Oxford: National Centre for Social Research.

Reading, N (2004) *Rosy and Jack: Innovative Resources*. Bendigo, Australia: Innovative Resources.

Reder, P, Duncan, S and Gray, M (1993) *Beyond Blame: Child Abuse Tragedies Revisited*. Hove: Routledge.

Reed, M and Canning, N (eds) (2010) *Reflective Practice in the Early Years*. London: Sage.

Rentzou, K and Ziganitidou, K (2009) Greek male early childhood educators: self and societal perceptions towards their chosen profession, *Early Years: International Research Journal*, 20 (3): 271–9.

Rodgers, C (2002) Defining reflection: another look at John Dewey and reflective thinking, *Teachers College Record*, 104 (4): 842–66.

Rowling, JK (2000) *Harry Potter and the Goblet of Fire*. London: Bloomsbury.

Rubin, KH, Fein, G and Vandenberg, B (1983) Play, in Hetherington, EM (ed.), *Handbook of Child Psychology*: Vol. 4. *Socialization, Personality, and Social Development*. New York: Wiley.

Rumbolt, A (1990) *The Rumbolt Report: Starting with Quality*. London: HMSO.

Rushforth, C (2012) *Safeguarding and Child Protection in the Early Years*. London: Practical Pre-School Books.

Sakellariou, M and Rentzou, K (2007) Male early childhood educators: the element missing from pre-school settings – a pilot study, *International Journal of Learning*, 14 (1): 41–50.

Samuelsson, IP and Johansson, E (2006) Play and learning – inseparable dimensions in pre-school practice, *Early Child Development and Care*, 176 (1): 47–65.

Save the Children (2012) *Child Poverty: It Shouldn't Happen Here*. Available at: **www.savethechildren.org.uk/ uk-child-poverty** (accessed 14 September 2012.

Schön, DA (1983) *The Reflective Practitioner*. New York: Basic Books.

Schön, DA (1994) *The Reflective Practitioner: How Practitioners Think in Action*. New York: Basic Books.

Schön, DA (1996) *Educating the Reflective Practitioner: Toward a New Design for Teaching and Learning in the Professions*. San Francisco: Jossey-Bass.

School Curriculum and Assessment Authority (1996) *Desirable Outcomes for Children's Learning on Entering Compulsory Education*. SCAA.

Scottish Executive (2001) *For Scotland's Children: Better Integrated Children's Services*. Edinburgh: TSO.

Shemmings, D and Shemmings, Y (2011) *Understanding Disorganised Attachment*. London: Jessica Kingsley.

Shemmings, D, Shemmings, Y and Cook, A (2012) Gaining the trust of 'highly resistant' families: insights from attachment theory and research, *Child and Family Social Work*, 17 (2): 130–7.

Shulman, L (1987) Knowledge and teaching: foundations of the new reform, *Harvard Educational Review*, 57 (1): 1–22.

Sidebotham, P, Atkins, B and Hutton, JL (2011) Changes in rates of violent child deaths in England & Wales between 1974 and 2008: an analysis of national mortality data, *Archives of Disease in Childhood*, 97 (3): 193–9.

Simon, B (1985) *Does Education Matter?* London: Lawrence & Wishart.

Simpson, D (2010) Being professional? Conceptualising Early Years professionalism in England, *European Early Childhood Education Research Journal*, 18 (1): 5–14.

Sinclair, R and Bullock, R (2002) *Learning from Past Experience: A Review of Serious Case Reviews*. London: Department of Health.

Siraj-Blatchford, I, Sylva, K, Muttock, S, Gilden, R and Bell, D (2002) *Researching Effective Pedagogy in the Early Years*, Research Report RR356. DCSF. Available at: **www.dfes.gov.uk/research/data/uploadfiles/ RR356.pdf**.

Skidmore, D (1996) Towards an integrated theoretical framework for research in special educational needs, *European Journal of Special Educational Needs*, 11 (1): 33–47.

Smith, PK and Vollstedt, R (1985) On defining play: an empirical study of the relationship between play and various play criteria, *Child Development*, 56 (4): 1042–50.

Smith, I, Brisard, E. and Menter, I (2006) Models of partnership developments in initial teacher education in four components of the United Kingdom: recent trends and current challenges, *Journal of Education for Teaching*, 32 (2): 147–64.

Spillane, JP (2005) Distributed leadership, *Educational Forum*, 69 (2): 143–50. Available at **http://dx.doi.org/ 10.1080/00131720508984678** (accessed on 10 August 2012).

Statistics New Zealand (2006) *Early Childhood Education*. Available at: **www.stats.govt.nz/browse_for_stats/ people_and_communities/pacific_peoples/pacific-progress-education/executive-summary.aspx** (accessed 29 June 2012).

Steiner Waldorf Schools Fellowship (2009) *Guide to the Early Years Foundation Stage in Steiner Waldorf Early Childhood Settings*. Forest Row: White Horse Press.

Stephen, C (2010) Pedagogy: the silent partner in early years learning, *Early Years*, 30 (1): 15–28.

Swaffield, S (2007) Light touch critical friendship, *Improving Schools*, 10 (3): 205–19.

Swick, K (2004) *Empowering Parents, Families, Schools and Communities During the Early Years*. Champaign, IL: Stipes Publishing.

Sylva, K, Melhuish, E, Sammons, P, Siraj-Blatchford, I and Taggart, B (2004) *Effective Provision of Pre-School Education*. Norwich: DfES Publications.

Taggart, G (2011) Don't we care? The ethical and emotional labour of early years professionalism, *Early Years*, 31 (1): 85–95.

Thomas, M (2001) *The Leadership Trust*. Available at: **www.leadership.org.uk/** (accessed September 2010).

Tickell, C (2012) *The Early Years: Foundations for Life, Health and Learning. An Independent Report on The*

Early Years Foundation Stage to Her Majesty's Government. London: DfE.

Todd, L (2007) *Partnerships for Inclusive Education*. London: Routledge

Turnell, A (2012) *The Signs of Safety*, Comprehensive Briefing Paper. Resolutions Consultancy. Available at: **www.signsofsafety.net/briefing-paper** (accessed 31 August 2012).

Turnell, A and Edwards, S (1999) *Signs of Safety: A Safety and Solution Oriented Approach to Child Protection Casework*. New York: W. W. Norton.

UNESCO (1994) *The Salamanca Statement on Principles, Policy and Practice in Special Educational Needs*. Available at: **www.unesco.org/education/pdf/SALAMA_E.PDF** (accessed on 30 June 2012).

United Nations Charter for the Rights of the Child (1991) Available at: **www.unicef.org.uk/crc?gclid=CK_s-_LqlLUCFSHHtAodHTwABg&sissr=1** (accessed on 31 June 2012).

United Nations Charter for the Rights of the Child (1989) Available at: **www.unicef.org.uk/UNICEFs-Work/Our-mission/UN-Convention/** (accessed on 30 June 2012).

Van IJzendoorn, MH, Schuengel, C and Bakermans-Kranenburg, MJ (1999) Disorganized attachment in early childhood: meta-analysis of precursors, concomitants, and sequelae, *Development and Psychopathology*, 11 (2): 225–50.

Vine, P and Todd, T (2005) *Ring of Confidence – Building Resilience with Early Years*. Trowbridge, Wilts: Positive Press.

Vygotsky, LS (1978) *Mind in Society: The Development of Higher Psychological Processes*. Cambridge, MA: Harvard University Press.

Ward, U (2009) *Working in Partnership in Early Years Settings*. Exeter: Learning Matters.

Warnock, M (1978) Special Educational Needs. Report of the Committee of Enquiry into the education of handicapped children and young people. London: The Stationery Office.

Warnock, M (2005) *Special Educational Needs: A New Look*. London: Philosophy of Education Society of Great Britain.

Whalley, ME (2011) *Leading Practice in Early Years Settings*, 2nd edn. Exeter: Learning Matters.

Williams, I (2009) Offender health and social care: a review of the evidence on inter-agency collaboration, *Health and Social Care in the Community*, 17 (6): 573–80.

Williams-Siegfredson, J (2011) *Understanding the Danish Forest School Approach: Early Years Education in Practice (Understanding the Approach)*. London: Routledge.

Wilson, K (ed.) (2007) *Child Protection Handbook,* 3rd edn. Oxford: Ballière Tindall.

Wood, E (2007) Reconceptualising child-centred education: contemporary directions in policy, theory and practice in early childhood, *FORUM*, 49 (1 and 2): 119–35.

Wood, E (2010) The play and pedagogy relationship, in Brooker, L and Edwards, S (eds), *Engaging Play*. Maidenhead: Open University Press.

Wood, E and Attfield, J (2005) *Play, Learning and Early Childhood Curriculum*. London: Paul Chapman.

WorkingTogetherOnline (2012). Available at: **www.workingtogetheronline.co.uk/consultation/contents.htlm#work** (accessed on 10 March 2013).

Zins, JE, Weissberg, RP, Wang, MC and Walberg, HJ (eds) (2004) *Building Academic Success on Social and Emotional Learning: What Does the Research Say?* New York: Teachers College Press.

Index